*Bob McNally's* Complete Book
*Of* ......................

# Fishermen's Knots, Fishing Rigs, And How To Use Them

## By Bob McNally

McNally Outdoor Productions

# Books By Bob McNally

Florida Fisherman's Handbook

Consumer's Guide To Fishing Tackle

On Camping

The Joy of Fishing

# Dedication

## To Tom McNally....

      The man who showed a little boy on Big Hunting Creek that the world was full of ripples and pools, darting brook trout, whippoorwill songs, and outdoor dreams that do come true.

Printed in the United States of America by
Atlantic Publishing Company
P.O. Box 67
Tabor City, N.C. 28463

Design and layout by
Mary E. Shelsby
Honeoye Falls, N.Y. 14472

Library of Congress Card Number 92-074447

ISBN Number 0-9646265-1-9

# About the Author . . .

**Bob McNally** is one of the most widely read and respected outdoor writers in a field rich with talent. He has fished throughout the world over the past 35 years, and has caught most of the globe's important sportfish, traveling an average of 50,000 miles annually pursuing fish for his stories and photographs.

He caught his first bass at age 3, first brook trout at 5, his first sailfish at age 9, first tarpon and steelhead at 10. His first magazine feature about fly-rod bass fishing was sold to *Sports Afield* at age 18.

McNally has written over 2,000 outdoor features for every important outdoor publication in America, including *Outdoor Life, Field & Stream, BassMaster* and *SaltWater Sportsman*. He is the author of nine books, and is on the writing staffs of *Southern Outdoors, Florida Sportsman* and *Fishing Facts* magazines. He has been a syndicated outdoor radio host, has appeared on many fishing television shows, and has done numerous fishing seminars around the country. His writing, broadcasting and photography work have won over 150 awards.

McNally lives near Jacksonville, Florida with his wife Chris, and three children Eric, Matt and Lindsey.

# Contents

Forward:                                         viii

Introduction:                                 xi

Knotty Problems                            1

Line-To-Line Knots                     11

Knots for Tying Lines to Hooks, Lures,
    Swivels Etc...                       49

Loops and Specialty Knots         117

Knots For Fly Fishing              139

Wire, Cable Connections          185

Knots In Everyday Fishing Rigs     203

Good Knots and Playing Fish Right   271

Index                                        279

# Foreword:

Knots hold the dubious honor of being the potentially weakest link in your tackle. There are few moments in angling as deflating as discovering the small pigtail of curled line and vanished hook that signals the failed knot that caused the loss of a good fish. Knots can cut themselves into nonexistence, too, so that we may at first blame line or leader rather than ourselves in choosing the wrong knot for a particular purpose or erring in some step while making the tie.

Frustrating as they can be, it is impossible to get along without knots. To further compound the situation, in order to enjoy the angling world's amazingly varied opportunities with different kinds of tackle, one truly needs a good repertoire of knots.

Few anglers have the good fortune to savor as many forms of sport fishing with the regularity enjoyed by author Bob McNally. His worldwide travel has resulted in continued use of the simplest to the most exotic constructions of terminal tackle. They are second nature to him, and therefore he is the natural choice to produce a book that describes in detail how to tie knots, and which to use under varying angling conditions and styles. Whether you need just a refresher or a complete foundation in the building of a knot you've never tied, you're sure to find it in these pages. Because the construction of certain specialized knots is often considered so difficult as to border on the metaphysical, you will be delighted that McNally's tying descriptions and illustrations are as clear as Stueben crystal. There is reason for this.

I am convinced that Bob McNally may have learned to tie a hook to a line before he learned to properly tie his shoe laces. I have on angling adventures to strange and wondrous places, seen him quickly and expertly help anglers become proficient with some esoteric and absolutely essential knot for the fishing at hand. I have watched him spin line or leader into intricate knots and practical fishing rigs like a snake charmer working a crowd.

There is good reason for the clarity and thoroughness of this unique knots and fishing rigs book. You do not garner the number of assignments, masthead positions, book credits, broadcast positions and awards as a journalist as Bob McNally has unless you are very good at your craft. And Bob is very, very good.

More than showing you how to tie virtually any knot you will ever need, McNally's subjects also encompass why various ties work when they do with different materials, and how to put knots to use building connections for myriad fishing assignments.

There is special satisfaction in watching a properly, neatly tied knot snug tightly and cleanly to its completion. It is matched by the confidence of knowing that you have made a connection that will not fail despite the best efforts of a strong-hearted fish. McNally's work will give you the knowledge to have that confidence.

**Jerry Gibbs**
Fishing Editor,
*Outdoor Life Magazine*

*When big fish are on the line quality knots are important.*

# Introduction:

One spring day a fishing guide watched an angler on North Florida's St. Johns River fight an enormous largemouth bass he had hooked with a plastic worm. After 10 minutes, the fisherman had the bass beaten, laying played out on its side beside the boat. The fisherman moved the huge bass toward an open landing net held by the guide. That's when the largemouth gave a final flop—and broke free. The angler insisted on tying his own knot that morning, and it had pulled loose at the hook.

"That was one of the biggest bass I'd ever seen," the guide remembers. "I'm sure the fish was 15 or 16 pounds. Tears welled up in the angler's eyes when he watched that bass swim away. I wanted to tie a good, reliable knot for the angler, but he said he could do it himself."

Another day, a fly fisherman drifted several nymphs he'd tied in tandem off leader "droppers" in the deep, swirling currents of Oregon's Deschutes River. As the flies drifted near bottom, the line suddenly paused as a steelhead struck one of the dropper flies. The angler set the hook and a 20-pound streak of chrome-sided, sea-run rainbow catapulted time-and-again across the river. For a few moments his limber fly rod bucked solidly against the fish, then the line went slack, and the steelhead bounced away downstream. The knot connecting the dropper line to the leader tippet didn't hold, and the saddened fisherman lost the trout of a lifetime.

Still another day, an angler in a center-console boat was trolling off North Carolina for king mackerel. Kings were abundant that day, but they were elusive. The fish constantly struck live and dead baits "short," taking only the rear half of baits and missing the hooks the angler had positioned in the noses of the baits. The fisherman didn't know how to fasten a second or third hook with wire in tandem to his bait rigs, so caught no mackerel—while other anglers who employed tandem-hook rigs landed many kingfish weighing to 30 pounds.

These three examples of outsize fish lost because of knot failure, or not caught because of poor rigging skills, are typical of thousands of similar incidents that occur around the world every year. Annually, many thousands of prized fish are lost because some angler did not tie a suitable knot;

*Casting perfection and stream knowledge are of no value if a knot pulls free or cuts itself when a fish strikes.*

or improperly tied the correct knot; or was unable to rig lures and baits the right way because he didn't know the knots or wire wraps needed. The sad part is there is no need for prize fish or even average fish to be lost because of poor knots, or because anglers are unable to rig lures or baits in the manner needed to be successful.

For every angler, and most particularly for the serious angler, the ability to tie proper fishing knots is **vitally important**. It is one of the most critical factors to fishing success. When all other things are normal, a fisherman's knots are the weakest part of his equipment. More prize fish are lost because knots pull out, slip, or cut themselves than are lost because of a broken line or faulty tackle. Knot tying may be somewhat unimportant in fishing for panfish—but even panfishermen must utilize at least a rudimentary knot-tying system to effectively construct a line-leader-bobber-hook terminal rig. Moreover, in almost all other types of important fishing—such as angling for striped bass, pike, muskies, tarpon, redfish, billfish, etc.—skillful knot tying and rig making are the difference between simply hooking fish or **hooking fish and landing them!**

There are hundreds of good knots that can be used by fishermen. And many fishermen consider it a measure of angling skill if they're the master of several dozen different kinds of knots. The average angler under average fishing conditions—whether he employs bait, spinning, or fly tackle—need know only a handful of knots. Even the most experienced anglers, those who use different tackle under different conditions in different places, frequently utilize only a dozen or so knots—even though they know how to tie most knots of angling value. For example, fully 50 percent of the fishing situations that arise can be taken care of by the fisherman who knows how to tie an Improved Clinch Knot, Blood Knot, Surgeon's Knot, Bimini Twist and Nail Knot. However, there are many dozens of different knots—and wire wraps—and **under certain circumstances each knot is extremely valuable.** Thus, the skilled and consistently successful angler can tie many different knots!

Fishermen should know that most knots reduce line strength at least to some extent—how much depends upon the knot you use and how carefully you tie it. For example, when you tie nylon line to a lure with the Improved Clinch Knot, you reduce the strength of the line by about 5 percent. If you tie the knot carelessly, it reduces the strength of the line even more (putting only five turns in an Improved Clinch Knot is important because four turns decreases the knot's strength substantially. Six turns gives less strength than five, and seven are worse than six).

The average quality knot, however, when properly tied, should reduce line strength no more than 10 percent, and the best knots will give 100 percent of the stated line strength. The strength of the knots you use, and how well you consistently tie them, makes a significant difference in your fishing success when several knots are used together in forming a fishing rig. Tie one knot incorrectly, or choose the wrong knot or wire wrap for a specific purpose in the rig, and the entire "system" can fail under the pressure of fighting a good fish.

Although most knots will reduce a line's strength somewhat, there are some knots so bad they never should be used by fishermen under any circumstances. No such knots are listed in this book.

Also, it must be realized that monofilament line, when bent over on itself at certain angles, is **self cutting**. Thus, knots such as the Figure Eight, Half-Hitch, and Double Half-Hitch, are cutting knots, and therefore should be avoided whenever possible by the angler.

*For every angler, and most particularly the serious angler, the ability to tie proper fishing knots and use them to make effective rigs, is vitally important to success.*

When learning to tie a knot, it is best to practice with heavy cord, heavy monofilament or braided line, light rope, or even a discarded fly line —rather than with light fishing line. The heavier material will show more clearly how the knot is shaped and formed, and once the beginner learns how to tie a knot with heavy material, he then can tie it readily with standard fishing lines.

When knots aren't tied properly, the most expensive fishing tackle is useless. Even casting perfection, and stream or fish knowledge are of no value if a knot pulls free or cuts itself when a fish strikes. So all fishermen should make every effort to learn to tie knots skillfully, and it is hoped that this book will help to make that task simpler.

An attempt has been made in **FISHERMEN'S KNOTS** to eliminate the confusion that comes with many various names for the same knot. Some popular knots are known under a variety of names. So as many of the common names as possible are listed for each knot.

When fishing, you may want to keep this book in your tackle box, fishing jacket pocket or boat compartment so you can quickly refer to it when some knotty angling problem arises. Also, you may find it beneficial to review certain chapters or certain knots or rigs from time to time, especially when faced with a new fishing experience—such as fishing for tarpon or deep walleyes for the first time.

This book is a greatly updated and expanded revision of a

book I did with my father, Tom, in 1975. That book, was created after many anglers requested more knot and rig making information after an extensive chapter on knots and rigs first appeared in the **FISHERMAN'S BIBLE**, published in 1970. The first **FISHERMEN'S KNOTS** book was the **first and only** knot-tying guide allowing for easy stream, lake, ocean and bayside reference to the tying of **all** known knots of practical value to fishermen.

This new book is better. There are many more new knots included here, and the rigs they are shown with are among the best and most advanced anglers are employing today. The nearly 200 knots and rigs in this book are useful to all anglers, regardless of whether they are stillfishermen, spin fishermen, bait-casters, trollers or fly fishermen, and regardless of whether they fish in freshwater or saltwater, inshore or offshore. In addition, all the knots and rigs in this book have been proven not only scientifically via machine testing, but—and perhaps of more importance—they have been tested over many years under actual and varied fishing conditions.

It's my hope that you'll find this book instructive and helpful, and that it will aid you in bringing to net and gaff many more fish, and especially those trophy fish that, otherwise, might have been just another tale about the one that got away!

**—Bob McNally**

*Nylon monofilament must be tied very carefully to secure properly, which is important when fishing for heavy largemouth bass.*

# ① Knotty Problems

Fishermen today have many more knot-tying problems than did fishermen years ago. The "age of synthetics" has made it necessary for all anglers to become skilled at knot tying.

In other days, fishermen had lines and leaders made of "natural" materials, silk fly lines, for example, silkworm gut leaders, lines braided of linen, etc. Today, virtually all fishing lines and leaders are of man-made materials, chiefly nylon. Many knots that were useful with old natural material lines/leaders are unsatisfactory with today's synthetic lines/leaders. The synthetics have finishes about as smooth as glass, so some knots tied in them slip readily, and therefore are useless.

Excluding metal lines, most modern fishing lines are braided Dacron, braided nylon or nylon monofilament. Dacron is a fine-diameter line with little stretch, and is used primarily for trolling, chiefly in saltwater. Braided-nylon lines are popular among anglers using revolving-spool reels, in both freshwater and saltwater. Braided nylon is soft, spools nicely, is water repellent, and it wears well.

But monofilament is the most popular and versatile fishing line for just about all angling conditions. It can be made specifically for any type fishing, varying in elasticity, abrasion resistance, suppleness, hardness, etc. Thus today's monofilament is available in many different designs for virtually any fishing situation. There are, for example, monofilaments designed for saltwater, others made for ice fishing, some expressly for use on spinning reels, others made solely for fly leaders.

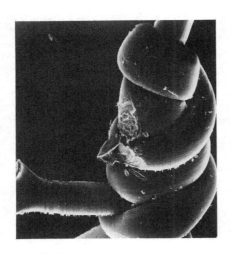

*This close-up photogaph of an Improved Clinch Knot trimmed too close with clippers shows how easily a knot can be damaged. Even minor damage in a knot can weaken it substantially, and cost an angler an important fish.*

All monofilaments, however, fully tax the angler's knowledge of knots, and his ability to tie them. Nylon monofilament line must be tied very carefully to be secured properly. In knots where the friction is against

**2**

material other than monofilament itself, the knot has a tendency to slip. But in knots where the friction is chiefly on the monofilament itself, there is less chance for the knot to slip, break or untie.

Four basic steps should be taken in tying any knot correctly. The knot should be formed or shaped, then drawn, next tightened, and finally, trimmed and checked.

The first step—forming or shaping a knot—is vital. A knot that isn't formed correctly will not "draw up" properly, nor will it tighten as it should. Build or "form" each knot slowly and carefully, being sure each turn is made as it should be, each loop is in proper place, and so on. "Forming" a good fishing knot is much like forming the bow knot used to tie your shoes. If formed carefully, a shoe knot can be drawn up

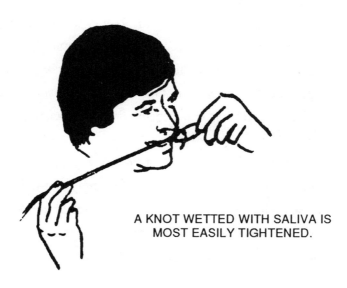

A KNOT WETTED WITH SALIVA IS
MOST EASILY TIGHTENED.

properly, tightened, then checked, and your shoes won't untie. If the shoe bow is not formed carefully, and isn't drawn up correctly, a poor knot is the result and it won't remain secure.

After a fishing knot has been formed satisfactorily, it should be "drawn up" slowly, just like your shoe bow knot. Don't yank on the fishing knot ends, or on the line/leader material. Instead, pull the fishing line "tag" ends evenly and gently, so all components of the knot remain in their proper places and fit together snugly. A steady, even pressure should be used in "drawing up" the knot.

A knot can be drawn more easily if it is wetted with saliva or water. Both act as lubricants that help knot components slide smoothly into place. Also, a thumb nail can be used to push the turns of a knot together until they are seated securely.

To tighten a knot, pull firmly and steadily on the "standing" parts, as well as on all ends. As much pressure should be applied as the line will take without breaking. It is not possible to tighten a knot too much. Any knot that isn't tightened correctly is going to slip under sufficient pressure, and may break or pull free.

It's easy to cut hands or fingers when tightening knots, especially with monofilament. Surprisingly, the finer diameter the mono, the more readily it cuts. A handkerchief wrapped around the hand or fingers will prevent mono cuts when tightening knots, or light gloves may be worn.

**4**

Knots in heavy material can be tightened with pliers, or by wrapping the line around a shoe or boat cleat, and pulling firmly with both hands. Another way to tighten a knot fastened to a fly or lure, is to attach the hook to a metal ring that is well seated—a screw eye or boat cleat, for example. Then pull on the standing line and the knot's tag end to tighten it securely. On a boat, a short length of 100-pound test monofilament can be tied around a hand rail or large cleat to produce a secure loop for tightening knots on lures and hooks. Into the mono loop a hook is fitted for secure "holding," while the knot is safely tightened.

When tightening a knot that is connected to a fly or lure, be careful to keep fingers away from the hook. Many fishermen have buried hooks in their fingers and hands be-cause the lure slipped during the tightening process as the knot was drawn tight.

The final step in knot tying, or knot "building," is checking or testing the completed knot. No experienced angler ever ties a knot and then starts fishing. He checks a new knot carefully before making his first cast.

In checking a knot, first take a good look at it to see if it appears right. Many improperly tied knots look just that way—like improperly tied knots. If you notice a turn in the knot hasn't pulled into place exactly right, that there's an unwanted "hump" in the knot, or some other deficiency, cut the knot off and tie another. If you don't, it could cost you the fish of a lifetime, all because you didn't take the extra couple minutes to retie.

If a knot looks right, test it by pulling against it with whatever pressure the line or leader will bear. Pull on both sides of the knot, if it is a knot joining lines.

If the knot you've tied connects to a hook, fly or lure, attach the hook to a screw eye or something similar and pull hard on the fishing line. If it's a different kind of knot, such as line-to-line, you can check it by wrapping part of the line around a soft-soled shoe and pulling on it.

**ALWAYS INSPECT A KNOT FOR FLAWS PRIOR TO FISHING WITH IT.**

Never test a knot by a sudden jerk or yank on the line. Perfectly good lines and knots can be popped by giving them sudden, powerful jolts. Neither lines or knots are made to withstand that sort of abuse.

After completing a knot, trim its "tag ends" as close to the knot as possible. Many fishermen do not trim excess tag ends of a knot closely because they fear the knot may pull out. Any knot that is properly tied can be trimmed very close and it will not pull out or loosen.

Tag ends of knots should be cut, **never** burned with a match or cigarette. Burning can weaken the knot or adjoining line. A sharp knife, razor or scissors can be used to trim knots closely. The best tool for knot trimming is a pair of nail clippers. Heavy-duty clippers designed specifically for fishing are good, but toe-nail clippers work well, too. Such clippers readily cut the heaviest monofilament and other lines, and they can be used to trim knot tag ends very closely. Some well-made fishing pliers also have good cutters that work great for knot trimming, especially heavy monofilament. It seems obvious, but most clippers are not designed for cutting wire. Yet many anglers regularly ruin nail clippers and even side-cutter pliers by using them on wire. Only specially-designed

NEVER TRIM A KNOT WITH A MATCH OR
CIGARETTE, AS THAT CAN DAMAGE THE
LINE.

tools clip wire without damaging their cutting edges.

Many beginners at knot tying compound their problems by never allowing themselves enough line or leader material with which to easily tie a knot. Fishing lines and nylon monofilament leader material are inexpensive, so there is no reason to skimp on line when tying a knot. Always allow at least eight or 10 inches of line to work with when tying a knot, and some knots require more line than that if they are to be formed quickly and correctly. By allowing plenty of line with which to tie a knot, the knot will be formed well, it will draw up properly and, more importantly, you'll be able to tie any knot quickly and perfectly.

Veteran anglers always check their lines and leaders before tying a knot. The line or leader that has abrasions, nicks or other weak spots should be discarded. The best knot tied into such a line/leader is useless, since the line/leader is going to part under pressure.

It's difficult to tie decent knots in monofilament that's kinked or "curly." Line left on reels for long duration often are curly, and fly fishing leaders frequently are full of "kinks."

The best way to straighten kinky monofilament is to run it between the folds of a rubber square, over a section of rubber hose, around the ankle of rubber waders, or under the sole of **clean** rubber-sole shoes. The friction caused by rubbing monofilament briskly against rubber will straighten line. Be sure, however, that the shoe, boot, etc. is **spotlessly**

**8**

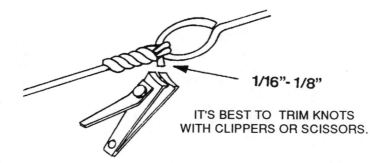

1/16"- 1/8"

IT'S BEST TO TRIM KNOTS
WITH CLIPPERS OR SCISSORS.

**clean,** or sand or dirt might fray the monofilament.

Another way to "get the kinks out" of monofilament is to pull line from the reel, 50 to 100 feet is about right. Then have someone hold the line end while you pull on the line steadily and firmly. This "stretching" process helps take "memory coils" out of line.

Some savvy fishing guides have pre-cut leaders handy during fishing, such as heavy-test monofilament shock tippets. They store leaders inside 1/2-inch diameter lengths of PVC pipe, cut to the desired length of leaders. To make pre-cut mono leaders perfectly straight, with no kinks for easy knot tying, place them in a large pan of water warmed on a stove. The water isn't boiling, but it's hot enough to "unkink" the mono leaders, which then are stored perfectly straight and ready for fishing in the PVC pipe, secured at each end with cork stoppers.

*Hard-fighting smallmouth bass tax an angler's knots to their fullest.*

# Line-To-Line
# Knots

The need for knotting two fishing lines together is an everyday occurrence in the world of angling. Some fishermen use the proper knots for this job, but most don't.

This chapter illustrates and explains the many different knots that have been designed for the specific purpose of connecting one line to another.

One such knot is the Blood Knot. It is world famous for tying together two pieces of nylon monofilament line that are of **nearly equal diameter**. The Blood Knot is a good one, but it won't do everything. For example, it isn't an appropriate knot for tying 60-pound test monofilament to 12-pound test mono. Instead, a Shocker Knot or Albright Special should be used to join lines of such varying diameters.

Under various fishing conditions, each knot presented in this chapter is of special value to anglers at one time or another. All known knots that dependably connect fishing lines are included—this means knots specifically designed for

**11**

joining nylon monofilament, braided lines and fly lines. Knots and connections for wire are covered in another chapter.

Explanations are given in this chapter on how, why and when a particular knot should or should not be used to join lines.

## DROPPER KNOT

This is a good knot for tying a dropper line to a leader or other line when an Extension Blood Knot isn't practical. When the Dropper Knot is "jammed" against a knot in the leader or line, as shown, it makes a small connection that readily runs through rod guides.

**Fig. 1** Lay the leader or line and the dropper line side-by-side. Wrap the dropper line around the leader three times, then push dropper line end back through the first loop.

**Fig. 2** Pull the knot tight, trim its ends, and the finished knot looks like this.

## FISHERMAN'S BEND KNOT

This is an excellent knot for joining two lines of equal diameter. However, it is not an easy knot to tie, and other knots such as the Blood Knot, are more often used.

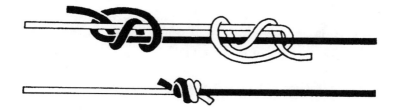

## LEADER KNOT

This knot is an excellent one for tying two monofilament lines together, and some experts believe it's much easier
to tie than the Blood Knot.

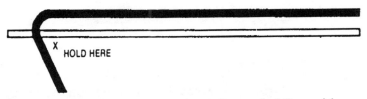

**Fig. 1** Lap the ends of the stands as shown, holding with
thumb and forefinger where marked.

**Fig. 2** Loop end around both lines and poke it through all
three loops.

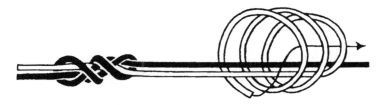

**Fig. 3** Now twist the other end around both strands three
times and stick the end through all three loops.

**14**

**Fig. 4** When both sides of the knot look like this, slowly pull it tight using your fingernails to push the loops together.

**Fig. 5** Finished knot looks like this.  Trim ends close.

## VARIATION OF FISHERMAN'S BEND KNOT

Some anglers still use this variation because the ends of the knot are in the center of the tie, and the knot passes through rod guides easily. Although it's much easier to tie this knot than the standard Fisherman's Bend, there are other knots for joining lines of equal diameter that can be tied faster.

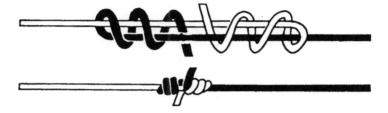

## TRIPLE FISHERMAN'S BEND KNOT

This is just an improved version of the Fisherman's Bend Knot. It is used for joining two strands of nylon monofilament and is a good knot for making fly leaders. Although it does take some practice to tie properly, it is a superb connection.

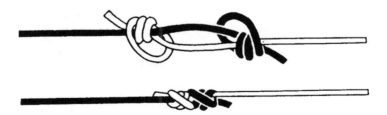

## MULTIPLE CLINCH KNOT

This is a good knot for bait-casters who use monofilament leaders six or eight feet long, because they need a knot
joining leader to line that isn't bulky. This knot passes from
reel through rod guides easily, and is extremely strong.

## SHOCKER KNOT

This is an excellent knot for tying together two lines of greatly different diameters. It's a strong, reliable, easy-to-tie knot that can be used for fastening lines as light as 10-pound test to ones testing 100-pounds or more.

**Fig. 1** Make an Overhand Knot in the light line end. Form a loose Overhand Knot in the heavy line and pass the end of the light line through the Overhand Knot.

**Fig. 2** Tighten the Overhand Knot.

**Fig. 3** Make three to five wraps with the light line around the heavy line, and pass the end back through the first loop. Pull on the light line ends until the wraps jam against the Overhand Knot in the heavy line. Then firmly pull on all line ends and trim close.

**18**

## ANGLER'S KNOT

**(Also called Single Fishermen's Knot)**

This is an excellent, quick-to-make knot for tying a dropper line to a leader. It's very popular with fly fishermen, but it's also useful for bait-casters and spin fishermen who want to fish two or more lures at the same time. The Angler's Knot is simple to tie. Just make two Overhand Knots, each around the standing part of the other line.

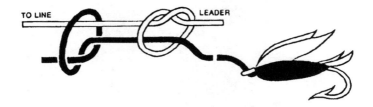

## VARIATION OF THE ANGLER'S KNOT

This connection is simply a regular Angler's Knot carried one step farther. The extra tie in the knot makes it more secure than an ordinary Angler's Knot.

*Heavyweight striped bass are found in many areas throughout the country, and make short work of terminal tackle with poorly-tied knots.*

## TILLER HITCH KNOT
**(Also called Tiller Knot, Slipped Hitch, Hitch Knot and Helm Knot)**

This old and reliable sailor's knot is a very good one for fastening a nylon leader to braided bait-casting line. This knot is useful because it can be untied easily, yet holds well when pulled tight.

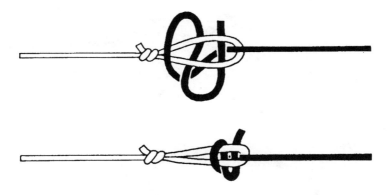

## BLOOD KNOT

This knot is valuable to all fishermen, particularly fly fishermen who use it to join nylon strands in making tapered leaders. Its only drawback is that the nylon strands to be connected must be of equal, or nearly equal, diameters— though 10-pound test can be tied to 20-pound using the Blood Knot. The Blood Knot provides a small connection, and when properly tied it cannot pull loose no matter how close its ends are clipped.

**Fig. 1** Cross the two lines, and wrap one line three times around the other. Now place the line end through the loop formed by the two lines.

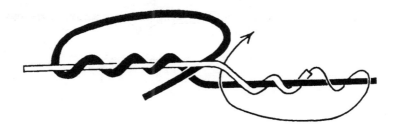

**Fig. 2** Turn the other line around the first line three times, put its end through the loop from the opposite side.

**Fig. 3** The turns should look like this. Now slowly pull on both long ends of the lines.

**Fig. 4** The tightened knot looks like this, loose ends trimmed.

## IMPROVED BLOOD KNOT

This is a superb knot for joining two lines of different diameters, like tying 12-pound test to 80-pound test. Simply double back the strands of the lighter line, and tie the knot. Also, this is a good-quality knot for tying a looped line formed by a Bimini Twist or Spider Hitch to a single strand of heavy shock tippet.

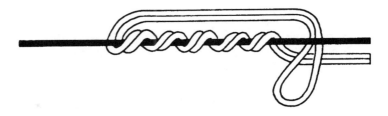

**Fig. 1** Wrap the doubled line five times around the larger diameter line and bring it back between the two strands.

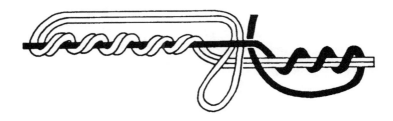

**Fig. 2** Twist the larger diameter line around the doubled line three times, and place its free end back through the loop in the opposite direction.

**Fig. 3** Pull the knot slowly to tighten it. Use your fingernails to push the knot loops together. Trim loose ends close.

*When huge bass are on the line in heavy cover, anglers must have complete confidence in the knots they tie.*

**25**

## ANOTHER IMPROVED BLOOD KNOT

This version of the Blood Knot is bulkier than the original Blood Knot. However, it's easy to tie and is a good connection for joining monofilament line. It is extremely important to form and tighten this knot well for it to have the best possible strength. Wetting the knot aids greatly in tightening.

## EXTENSION BLOOD KNOT

This knot is primarily used by fly fishermen who want to fish two flies simultaneously. Several blood knots can be

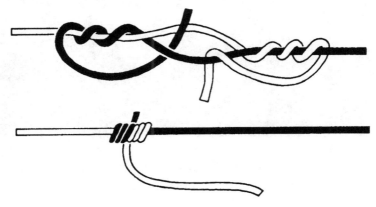

tied in a leader, then two, three, four or more flies can be tied on. It achieves the same results as all of the so-called "dropper knots," yet this one is **exceptionally** strong. A normal Blood Knot is tied and only one of the knot ends is trimmed. The dropper fly is tied to the untrimmed knot end. One tip to using this knot with several flies or lures is to keep dropper lines short. Dropper lines just 6- to 12-inches long help prevent tangling.

*The author was able to catch this near-record 72-pound roosterfish on 20-pound plug tackle because of a reliable knot system.*

## SIMPLIFIED BLOOD KNOT

Some anglers find the standard method of tying a Blood Knot complicated and difficult to handle. For these anglers, this method of making the Blood Knot may be easier.

**Fig. 1** Take the two line ends and tie a simple Overhand Knot, clipping the two tag ends.

**Fig. 2** Form a loop where the two lines meet, with the Overhand Knot at the bottom of the loop.

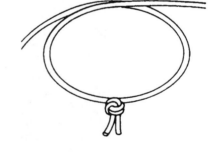

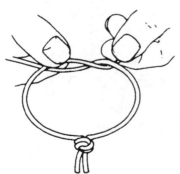

**Fig. 3** Begin making turns with the side of the loop having the Overhand Knot around the opposite side of the loop.

**Fig. 4** After six turns, reach through the center opening of the turns and pull the overhand knot through.

**Fig. 5** Hold the loop, while pulling tightly on both ends of the line, which jams the knot turns.

**Fig. 6** Clip off the loop and Overhand Knot, which produces a trim line-to-line connection that passes through rod guides easily.

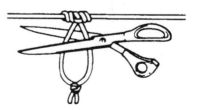

## JAM KNOT

**(Also called Pinch Jam)**

All of the following Jam Knots are used chiefly for joining a line to a loop, such as a fly line to a leader, or backing line to fishing line. They are very practical knots for joining almost any kind of lines, but the fisherman must be careful to tie the Overhand Knot very well before pulling the Jam Knot tight.

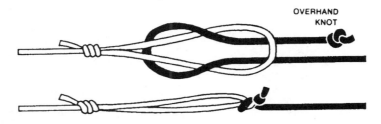

## JAM KNOT—SECOND METHOD

**(Also called Jam Hitch)**

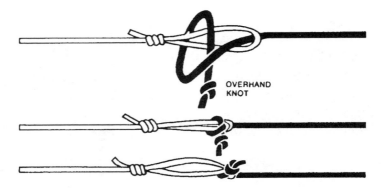

## JAM KNOT—THIRD METHOD

## SURGEON'S KNOT
**(Also called Double Water Knot and Joiner Knot)**

Many skilled anglers consider this the best and quickest knot for joining two lines of greatly varying diameters. It is primarily used by light-tackle anglers who need "shock leaders" for toothy fish such as northern pike, or fish that live in tough tangles like snook.

The Surgeon's Knot should be formed slowly and carefully, then drawn up and tightened evenly with all tag ends having steady pulls. It's best to moisten the knot, then pull **all four loose ends** of the knot evenly and smoothly until it's tight. Done correctly, the Surgeon's Knot can be used to secure 6-pound test to 60-pound test.

SHOCK LEADER

TO REEL

**31**

## FIGURE-EIGHT KNOT

This knot is sometimes used in emergency situations to join a leader to line. The knot is easy to tie and untie. However, it has low breaking strength and should only be used when it is not practical to tie a better knot, such as a Nail Knot or a Surgeon's Knot.

## KNOT FOR ATTACHING LEADER TO LINE

This knot is popular among fishermen who find it difficult to tie the Nail Knot, yet want a knot that will go through rod guides easily. The knot takes some practice, but it's easy to tie and very strong.

**Fig. 1** Lay the line and leader side by side. Wrap one line around the other strand twice, then poke the end around back through the two loops. Follow the same procedure when tying the second knot.

**Fig. 2** When the two loose ends have been trimmed, the finished knot looks like this. Tied properly, the knot will pass through rod guides well.

---

## TUCKED SHEET BEND KNOT

This is a safe and easy knot for joining a leader to a line loop. The advantage of this knot is that it can be readily tied with any kind of line.

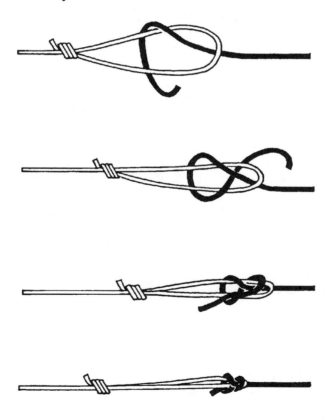

**33**

## LEADER DROPPER LOOP KNOT

This is a unique way to tie a dropper loop. Simply loop one end of a monofilament leader, lay it next to the other line, then tie a simple Overhand Knot leaving a large loop.

The Leader Dropper Loop is a good method of quickly and solidly tying a loop and leader to a fishing line. Trot line and bottom fishermen find this loop useful when making multi-hook rigs.

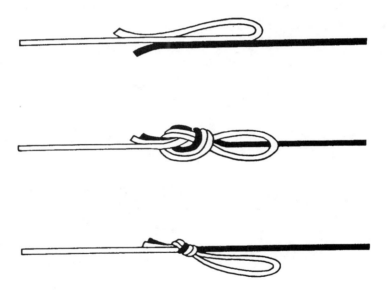

## DROPPER SNELL KNOT

This knot is used for tying dropper snells to a leader. The dropper line loop is held next to the leader, then the line end is put back through the loop and pulled tight.

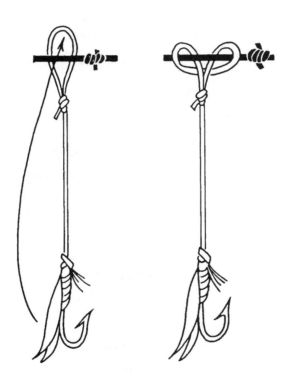

## OVERHAND DROPPER KNOT

This is a quick way of tying in a dropper line. The knot is simple to tie, but should be used only when more time cannot be used for another, better, knot.

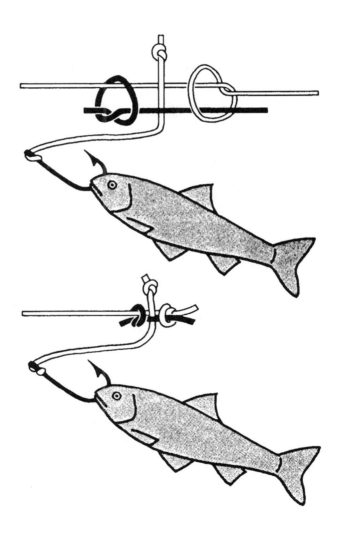

## BARREL KNOT

Although this is one of the best knots for joining lines of similar diameter, it's one of the most difficult to tie. The advantage of the Barrel Knot is that it is small, goes through rod guides with ease, and is very strong. Heavy monofilament or a fly line should be used when practicing this knot. With heavy mono or fly line it's easier to "form" and work the knot into place as it's being tightened.

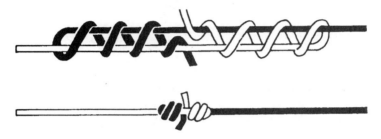

## EMERGENCY DROPPER KNOT

This is a fast, strong knot for tying dropper snells to a leader. This knot should only be used when it's impossible to tie the Extension Blood Knot.

**37**

## DOUBLE BECKET BEND KNOT

Although this is not the best knot for tying a line to a leader loop, it is quick and easy to tie. In an emergency, it can be of practical value to an angler.

## OVERHAND KNOT WITH A KNOTTED END

This is an extremely fast way to tie a heavy line to a leader loop. First put an Overhand Knot in the end of the heavy line and tighten it. Next pass the heavy line through the looped line, then tie another Overhand Knot in the heavy line.

## JOINING TWO LOOPS

This is a popular and good method of joining two looped lines, such as a fly line to backing line, or when building a specialized leader. It's main benefit is that leaders or lines can be changed quickly by utilizing such a loop-connection system. This is helpful when changing entire, pre-tied fly tippets, or when changing from a shooting head sinking fly line to a floating line.

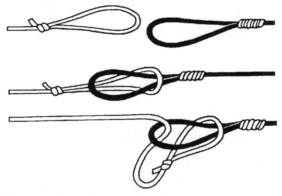

**Fig. 1** Pass one loop through the "eye" of the other loop. Then pull the entire remaining line through the loop.

**Fig. 2** When the loops are pulled tight they should connect like this.

**39**

## WOLF KNOT
### (Often called Wolf Splice)

This knot originated in Europe and for years it was the primary knot for anglers there connecting leaders. The Wolf Knot is a good secure tie, though often overlooked by American anglers.

## PENDRE DROPPER KNOT

The Pendre Knot is a good one for tying monofilament dropper lines to leaders. The knot is used often by fly fishermen, and originated in Switzerland.

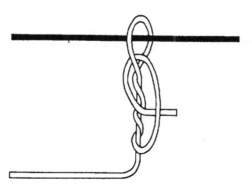

**Fig. 1** Wrap the dropper line around the leader. Make three turns around the standing part of the dropper line with the line end. Now pass the end through the first and last loops.

## WATER KNOT

This is a popular knot among bait-casters for tying breaks in braided line, or when attaching a monofilament leader to braided line. This knot also can be used for connecting monofilament, but it's not as secure as some knots like the Blood Knot.

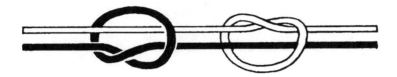

**Fig. 1** Tie two Overhand Knots, each around the standing part of the other line.

**Fig. 2** To improve the knot make several wraps around the standing part of each line, and poke the ends back through the loops.

## SINGLE WATER KNOT

The Single Water Knot is merely a simple Overhand Knot using both lines for the tie. It is not as secure as some similar knots, such as the Surgeon's. However, the Single Water Knot is fast and easy to tie.

## DOUBLE WATER LOOP KNOT
**(Sometimes called Double Fisherman's Knot)**

This knot was originally designed for tying gut leaders, however, some anglers still use the knot to satisfactorily join monofilament lines. The Double Water Loop Knot seems complicated, but it can be tied quickly and easily with practice.

## SNAKE DROPPER KNOT

This is a strong knot for tying a nylon dropper line to a leader or line. It's a popular knot among European anglers.

**Fig. 1** Place the dropper line beside the standing line. Make a loop in the dropper, and put its long end through the loop. Now make two turns, going around both the dropper line and the other strand.

**Fig. 2** Pull both ends of the dropper line to tighten the knot, then trim short end close.

## ALBRIGHT SPECIAL KNOT
### (Also known as Key Knot Splice and Key Loop)

This knot was made famous by the well-known Florida Keys guide Jimmy Albright, and is worthy to bear his name. It's an excellent knot for tying light test to heavy test line. It also can be used to connect line to wire cable, nylon-coated wire, and even to small diameter single-strand wire leader. When using wire, make certain the wire is used to make the single "loop" in the connection, while the multiple wraps are made with the more supple fishing line.

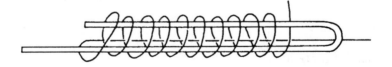

## COMPOSITE KNOT

This is a half Water Knot, half Jam Knot. It's used for tying heavy nylon "shock tippets" to light nylon when fishing for species such as tarpon, pike, roosterfish, billfish, etc. It's vitally important to "form" this knot correctly, then to tighten it and check it thoroughly before fishing. When tied well, this knot can be used to securely fasten lines of widely varying diameters, such as 10-pound test to 100-pound test.

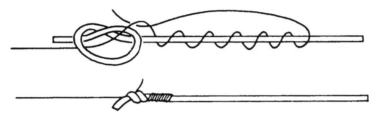

## SQUARE KNOT
### (Also called the Reef Knot)

This is a commonly used boating knot. It is a fast, efficient means to join two lines that are of equal diameter.

The knot is very reliable when all line ends are tied securely, and when there is equal tension on both lines.

**45**

## UNI-KNOT

This outstanding, versatile and durable knot was developed by renowned outdoor writer and angler Vic Dunaway. The Uni-Knot is more than a simple fishing knot, it is an entire knot-tying system. Here it's shown used to connect two fishing lines. It can be used to secure lines of light or heavy test, as well as light lines to heavy ones, or even doubled lines to shock tippets.

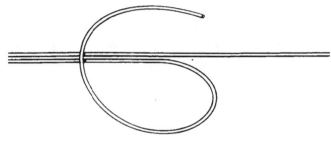

**Fig. 1** Overlap the ends of two lines for about 6 inches. With one line end form a circle, crossing the two lines about midway of the overlapped distance.

**Fig. 2** Make four turns with the tag end through the loop.

**Fig. 3** Pull the tag line end tight to jam the wraps of the Uni-Knot around the standing line.

**Fig. 4** Follow steps two and three with the opposite line end, then pull the knots together as tightly as possible.

**Fig. 5** Pull the standing lines in opposite directions to slide knots together. Pull tight and trim tag ends.

*Panfishermen—including youngsters Matt and Lindsey McNally—have great need for knowing what knots to use with their bait rigs.*

**48**

# 3 Knots for Tying Lines to Hooks, Lures, Swivels Etc...

Regardless of what kind of angling is at hand, with what kind of tackle, or where the fishing is done, an angler must join his fishing line to some sort of connecting ring. He may be tying his line directly to the "eye" of a hook, or to the ring of a lure or swivel, and so on. But he will need one or more of the knots presented in this chapter.

Knots tied to connecting rings most often are the ones that break or pull out when fighting fish. So the knot joining fishing line or leader to the lure, swivel, etc. is one of the most important in any knots system. Therefore, it should be tied carefully and deliberately.

Some special-purpose knots are included in this chapter, but most of the following knots are applicable to everyday fishing problems. Moreover, it pays to be able to tie a variety of knots for connecting line to hooks, lures and so on.

For example, an Improved Clinch Knot normally is adequate for joining fishing line to lure or hook. However, if very heavy monofilament line is used, it is almost impossible to tie an Improved Clinch Knot because heavy mono resists being tightened. A good knot for heavy mono is the Palomar Knot, but a large ring-eye must be used when tying the Palomar. If heavy mono must be tied to a small ring swivel or hook, another knot like the Homer Rhode Loop should be employed.

Experiment with these different knots, because all of them have applications for various types of fishing situations and knot tying problems.

---

## DOUBLE IMPROVED CLINCH KNOT

The Double Improved Clinch Knot is an extremely secure tie. However, it is difficult to make with heavy monofilament, and with braided lines, and it isn't practical with stout leaders. It is an ideal knot, however, with light-test lines, of under 10-pound strength. The knot is most often used by bass, trout and inshore saltwater anglers.

**Fig. 1** Double the line, bringing the line end back parallel to the standing line so there is about eight inches of double line. Take the end of the double line and push it through the hook eye. Wrap the doubled line end five times around the doubled standing part of the line, and push the line end back through the loop formed near the hook eye.

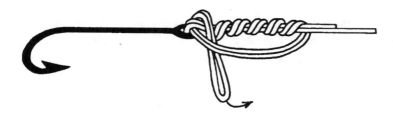

**Fig. 2** Pull the doubled line end through the loop in front of the hook eye, then push the end through the large loop, as shown.

**Fig. 3** Moisten the knot with saliva, then pull tight.

**51**

## DUNCAN LOOP KNOT
**(Also called Uni-Knot)**

       Here is an excellent "sliding loop" knot. When it's tied, it can be tightened anywhere on the standing part of the line, which means an angler can adjust the knot to form any size loop he desires. The loop will remain open during normal casting and retrieving. However, when a fish is hooked, the knot will slide down the line and "jam" tightly against the hook eye. After the fish is landed the knot can be moved up the line and the loop opened once again.

**Fig. 1** Put the line end through the hook eye, bringing about eight inches of line through the "eye" with which to tie the knot. Keep the line end parallel to the standing line.

**Fig. 2** Turn the line end down so it comes back underneath the two parallel strands. Wind the line end around the two parallel lines and through the loop, as shown.

**Fig. 3** Make five wraps around the two parallel lines, inside the loop. Then pull the tag end and standing part of the line to tighten the knot.

---

## DOUBLE-O KNOT
**(Often called Eye Knot)**

The Double-O Knot can be tied in a few moments, and it is a good knot to use with monofilament, braided line, and even nylon-coated wire. It is used by anglers who want a knot that can be tied quickly to "ring-eye" hooks and swivels.

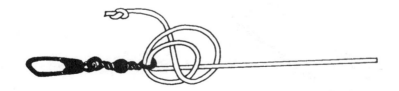

## PALOMAR KNOT

Many anglers find the Palomar Knot the easiest of all knots to use for tying line to hooks, lures and swivels. This is a strong, simple knot that can be tied just by "feel"—even in complete darkness. Because the line end must be doubled before making the Palomar, it can't be used for fastening heavy line or leaders to hooks or swivels with small rings.

**Fig. 1** Double the end of the line and pass the loop through the hook eye.

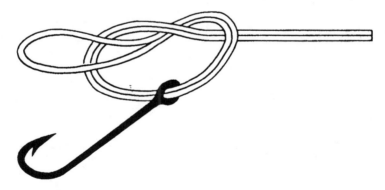

**Fig. 2** Double the loop back, then make an Overhand Knot around the standing line, leaving a loop large enough for the hook (or lure) to pass back through.

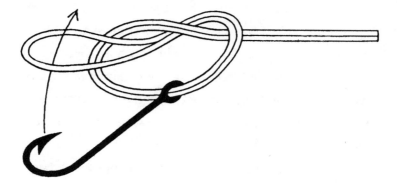

**Fig. 3** Put the entire hook (lure) through the loop, as illustrated.

**Fig. 4** Pulling on the standing line will draw the knot tight. Trim it, and the knot will be compact and effective.

## SERRURE KNOT

This knot looks much like several other knots, such as the Bumper Tie Knot. However, it is completely different and, moreover, it can be made with much heavier line.

The Serrure Knot was developed in France for tying monofilament to "flat-eye" hooks, and it's popular in parts of Europe. The knot seems impossible to tie the first time, but with practice it becomes quite easy.

Thread the end of the line through the hook eye, pulling about six inches of line through the "eye." Now lay the line that has been pulled through the hook eye parallel to the hook shank with your thumb and index finger, and bring the line end back toward the hook eye.

Now wrap the line end four times around the line and the hook shank, back towards the bend of the hook. Push the line end through the loop that the thumb and forefinger hold. Slowly pull on the standing part of the line in front of the hook eye, until the loop that the line end was put through is pulled tight and the knot "jams" behind the hook eye.

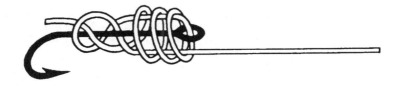

*This 12 1/2-pound largemouth bass was caught from a weedy lake thanks to a reliable knot system.*

## KING SLING

This knot is almost identical to the End Loop Knot, except the King Sling is used to create a loop at a lure's eye for better action during the retrieve. This is a very secure knot, that's fast to tie, but be sure to allow plenty of line to make a large, wide loop that will easily allow the lure to be passed through. It's best used with lines testing under 20-pounds.

**Fig. 1** Put the line end through the lure eye, then double the line, allowing about 10 inches of doubled line to tie the knot.

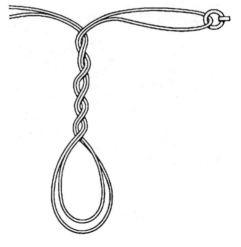

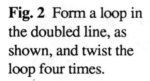

**Fig. 2** Form a loop in the doubled line, as shown, and twist the loop four times.

**58**

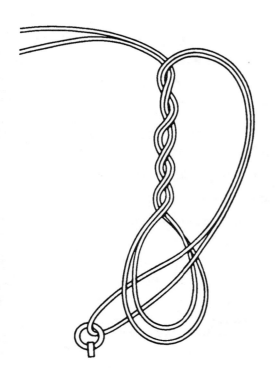

**Fig. 3** Put the lure through the large end loop in the doubled line.

**Fig. 4** Tighten the knot by pulling on the tag end, standing line, and the lure. Trim the knot tag end close.

## BUMPER-TIE KNOT

The Bumper Tie is popular with anglers who snell their own hooks, especially West Coast and Great Lakes fishermen who use spawn for salmon and trout. The Bumper Tie is a more complicated knot to make than the Snelling A Hook Knot, or the Quick Snell Knot. However, some fishermen prefer the Bumper Tie when using spawn sacks and some other natural baits, as they believe the tie can hold baits onto the hook better than other "snelling" knots, and the Bumper Tie is extremely strong.

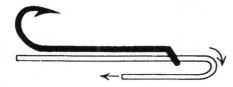

**Fig. 1** The leader end is pushed through the hook eye.

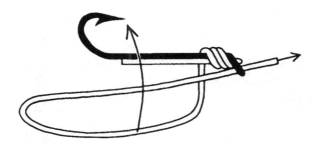

**Fig. 2** The standing part of the leader is wound three times around the hook shank and the leader end. Then the butt end of the leader is pushed out through the hook eye. The loop

formed by the butt end running out through the hook eye can be used to secure bait, like spawn sacks.

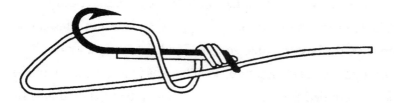

**Fig. 3** A loop of about four inches is left under the hook shank.

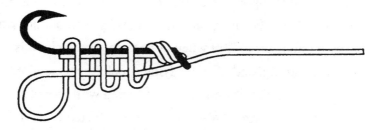

**Fig. 4** The loop is wrapped around the hook shank three times, forming a series of coils.

**Fig. 5** Now the standing part of the leader is slowly pulled tight, and the knot is completed.

## HOMER RHODE LOOP KNOT
### (Sometimes called Flemish Loop or Loop Knot)

This is an easy knot to tie, and very popular among marine and Midwest anglers who do considerable trolling. The Homer Rhode Loop allows plugs, spoons and other lures to have the best possible action. The knot forms a loop through the "eye" of a lure, so it "swims" more freely than if a knot were tied snugly to it. In fact, a loop formed by this knot often can make a diving plug run true that otherwise "tracks" irregularly.

The Homer Rhode Loop can be made with very heavy line, such as 100-pound test, making it a good line connection for marine jigs. Forming this knot carefully is important when heavy mono is used. But when done properly, the knot is extremely strong, and ideal for tying shock tippets to lures.

Although this knot is normally tied with monofilament or nylon-coated wire, it also can be used effectively with braided line.

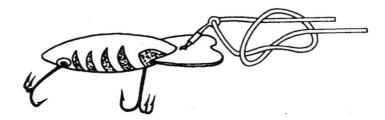

**Fig. 1** Tie a simple Overhand Knot about four inches from the end of the line. Push the end of the line through the hook eye, then back through the center of the Overhand Knot.

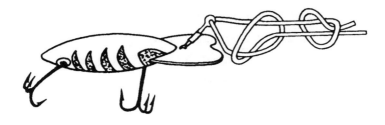

**Fig. 2** Next, with the end of the line, make another Overhand Knot around the standing part of the line. When tightened, the two Overhand Knots slide and jam together, meeting at the middle of the two loose Overhand Knots and forming a loop. Where the second Overhand Knot is positioned around the standing line determines the size of the knot's loop. For a big loop knot, form the second Overhand Knot well up the standing part of the line. For a small loop knot, make the second Overhand Knot close to the first Overhand Knot.

## BERKLEY TRILENE KNOT

**(Sometimes called Double-Loop Clinch Knot or Double Jam Knot)**

This is an excellent and easy-to-tie version of the standard Clinch Knot, which the Berkley Tackle Company researched and endorses for use with its monofilament. The Trilene Knot is somewhat new, and has only recently become popular among anglers who have learned of its remarkable strength.

This knot originally was popular with trollers, but has become very useful for light tackle anglers who demand 100 percent strength of their knots. It takes a bit more time to tie than the standard Clinch Knot, but for tarpon, muskie, salmon and pike fishermen, the Trilene Knot is a winner.

**Fig. 1** Turn the line end through the hook eye twice.

**Fig. 2** Wrap the line end around the standing part of the line three times, then put the line end back through the two loops in front of the hook eye.

**Fig. 3** The finished knot pulled tight.

*Knots in your leader better be tied correctly when tangling with tarpon.*

**65**

## IMPROVED BERKLEY TRILENE KNOT
### (Also Called Double Loop Improved Clinch Knot)

This is a Trilene Knot carried one step further. The line end is passed through the hook eye twice. The line is then wrapped several times around its standing part, then it is passed through the two loops near the "eye." The final step is to put the line end through the large loop, as shown.

The Improved Berkley Trilene Knot isn't difficult to tie. It's a very strong connection, especially with light-test line.

## SINGLE SHEET BEND KNOT

This is a suitable knot for taking panfish, and is occasionally used by anglers with heavy monofilament or nylon-coated wire—especially at night—because the knot is easy to form with heavy line or multi-strand wire.

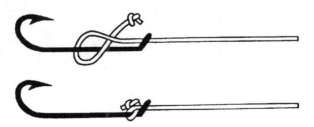

## COMPOUND KNOT

This knot is almost identical to the Perfection Loop, except that the knot forms a loop ahead of a hook, lure line-tie ring, or swivel.

The Compound Knot is difficult to tie for anglers with big hands and fingers, but with practice anyone can learn to tie it. The Compound Knot is great for making a loop at the lure or fly to provide more "swimming" action during the retrieve. The Compound Knot is an extremely durable connection with monofilament or braided line, and works well even with multi-strand wire.

**Fig. 1** Make a loose Overhand Knot about five inches from the line end. Pass the end of the line through the hook eye, then back through the center of the loose Overhand Knot. Wrap the line end over the standing part of the line just above the Overhand Knot, and push the line end between the two lines forming the Overhand Knot, as shown. Slowly pull the standing part of the line, the line end, and the hook or lure to tighten the knot. Tied and tightened correctly, the loop won't pull out, and the knot is as strong as the fishing line pound test.

**67**

## DOUBLE LINE HALF-HITCH KNOT

This knot is used often by saltwater anglers who need a simple tie for connecting heavy monofilament line to a hook, lure or swivel "eye." The Double-Line Half Hitch Knot, when tied properly and carefully, is adequate for light inshore saltwater fishing.

**Fig. 1** Double the line end so there's about six inches of "double-back" line with which to tie the knot. Next pass the doubled line through the hook or swivel "eye" twice. Tie two to four Half-Hitches with the end around the standing part of the doubled line.

**Fig. 2** This is the completed, tightened Double-Line Half Hitch Knot.

## BUFFER LOOP KNOT

This is a good "loop knot" for anglers who use heavy test shock tippets because it forms easily and quickly with stout monofilament. Nylon-coated, multi-strand wire also can be tied with this simple knot.

**68**

**Fig. 1** Tie an Overhand Knot about six inches from the end of the line, then pass the line end through the hook eye.

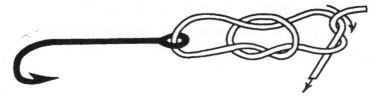

**Fig. 2** Put the line end back through the open Overhand Knot and tie a Half-Hitch with the line end onto the standing part of the line.

**Fig. 3** Now slide the Overhand Knot either up or down the standing part of the line. This will determine the size of the loop the knot will form. Slowly pull the line's end and its standing part to tighten the knot.

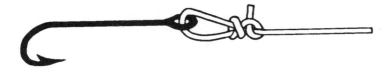

**Fig. 4** Trim the knot leaving a 1/8-inch tag end.

**69**

## BOW KNOT

The Bow Knot is simple and can be tied rapidly. Although it doesn't look like a secure knot, it is strong and reliable.

This knot can be used to fasten monofilament and braided lines to any type of connecting ring. It's also an especially good knot when used with medium-heavy mono lines testing to about 60 pounds.

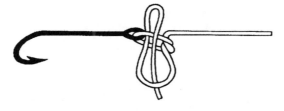

**Fig. 1** The hook eye is threaded with the line end and a loose Overhand Knot is tied. Now the line end is passed through the Overhand Knot, brought back over the knot and then pushed through the loop, as illustrated.

**70**

## ROUND-TURN FISH HOOK TIE

This knot is most often used by fishermen using heavy monofilament with natural baits. The knot holds best with stiff, heavy line. Also, the knot is most effective when there is a constant pull or pressure from the standing part of the line to the knot, as when trolling or stillfishing with a heavy bait or weight.

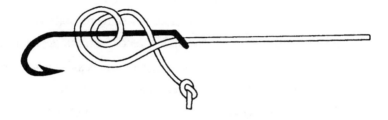

**Fig. 1** Thread the line through the hook eye. Make a wrap around the shank of the hook toward the hook eye, then tuck the line end under the wrap. Now tie an Overhand Knot in the end of the line.

**Fig. 2** Pull on the standing part of the line to tighten the knot.

## SNELLING A HOOK
### (Commonly called Salmon Hook Knot)

Generations ago Snelling A Hook was necessary because many hooks did not have "eyes." However, some expert anglers still insist today on snelling their "eyed" hooks because they feel snelling makes a strong, permanent connection. Also, a very direct, "hook set" in line with the plane of the hook is made when a fish is struck using this durable connection.

Snelled hooks often are used in fishing natural baits, especially for fish such as coho and Chinook salmon, steelhead, and when using live shiners for outsize largemouth bass in heavy cover.

Many bait fishermen prefer snelled hooks because bait can be slipped right over the leader knot. Also, with no knot on the leader above the hook, weeds and other debris are less likely to foul ahead of a bait on the line during fishing. This knot is easily made, and is very similar to the "whip finish" fly tiers use to secure thread when they've completed dressing a fly.

**Fig. 1** Thread the leader through the hook eye and lay the leader along the hook shank.

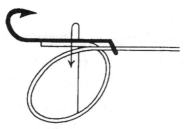

**Fig. 2** Pull about six inches of leader through the hook eye and form a loop below the hook shank, as shown.

**Fig. 3** Hold the line near its end tight and parallel to the hook shank, while wrapping the line loops (as shown) over the **entire hook**. Be sure the line of the loop closest to the hook eye forms the series of coils.

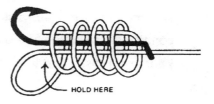

HOLD HERE

**Fig. 4** After six tight coils are formed on the hook shank, slowly pull on the standing part of the line. This will bring the rear loop through the coils and tighten the knot. At this point, bait such as spawn sacks can be firmly secured between the fishing line and hook shank, and held in place by the knot pulled tight and jammed against the hook eye.

**Fig. 5** The completed snell.

**73**

## McNALLY LOOP KNOT

Although there are some "loop knots" that may be stronger, such as the Nail Loop, this is one of the fastest and easiest to tie. It's most valuable to anglers who want a knot that forms a loop so their lures have good action during the retrieve. Also, this loop can be tied in seconds, making it useful to anglers who change lures frequently.

The McNally Loop is used by a wide cross section of anglers, from ice jiggers using gloves who need a simple lure connection; to tarpon and snook anglers who want a fast loop knot that's easily tied with stout line on large plugs.

**Fig. 1** Put the leader end through the lure's connecting ring, and double the line, leaving about eight inches with which to tie the knot.

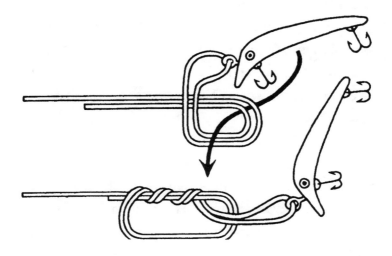

**Figs. 2 & 3** Pinch the end of the line against the standing part of the line. Now form a loop with the doubled line and make three Overhand Knots with the lure.

**Fig. 4** Pull the lure and the standing part of the line to tighten the knot.

## DOUBLE WEMYSS KNOT

The Double Wemyss Knot is not as good as some knots designed for turned-down hook eyes, such as the Double Turle Knot. However, this knot is fast to tie and untie, and is an adequate connection when a situation arises requiring that a knot be tied as speedily as possible.

The Double Wemyss Knot is easy to make. First, thread the line through the hook eye. Take the end of the line and loop it once around the standing line. Then double the end of the line back and wrap it twice around the standing line near the hook eye. Now take the first loop, slide it over the hook eye, and slowly tighten the knot so that the finished knot is on the hook shank behind the "eye."

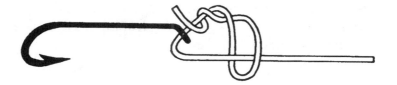

## IMPROVED CLINCH KNOT
**(Also known as Pandre Knot or Jam Knot With An Extra Tuck)**

The Improved Clinch Knot is one of the most popular knots for tying a line or leader to either a hook or lure eye. It is one of the most dependable and secure of all knots.

Although many anglers still insist on using the ordinary Clinch Knot, the Improved Clinch Knot is just as easy to tie, and it is much stronger.

The Improved Clinch knot can be difficult to tighten when using heavy-test monofilament of, say, over 40-pound. But if the tie is moistened well, even stout monofilament will tighten properly.

**Fig. 1** Pass the line end through the hook eye. Put about six inches of line through the eye so there will be ample line to tie the knot.

**Fig. 2** Hold the hook or lure securely in one hand and wrap the end of the line five times around the standing part of the line, as shown in the illustration. Now pass the line end back through the small loop near the hook eye, and also through the large loop.

**Fig. 3** Tighten and trim the knot carefully.

**77**

## NAIL LOOP KNOT

This is one of the best and most reliable knots for tying a loop to a fly or lure so it can "swim" or "wiggle" freely for best action.  Although the Nail Loop is more difficult to tie than some knots, such as the Homer Rhode Loop and Dave Hawk's Drop Loop, it's extremely strong and is highly recommended for rigging heavy-duty shock tippets as in sailfish and pike fishing.

**Fig. 1** Put the line end through the hook eye, leaving about eight inches with which to tie the knot.  Lay the line end parallel to the standing part and place a nail, tube, or toothpick between the two strands.  Then make 3 1/2-wraps with the end of the line back towards the hook eye.

**Fig. 2** Next slip the line end forward through the loops made by turning the line over the two parallel strands.

**Fig. 3** When this knot is tied carefully and the loops are pulled tight, the knot should look like this.

## TAUTLINE HITCH

This is a sliding loop knot that's easy to tie and valuable to any angler. When a Tautline Hitch is employed, a loop of any size may be formed, so that a lure will "wiggle" freely when retrieved. When a fish is hooked, the knot slides down and "jams" against the hook eye. After the fish is landed the knot can be opened again to re-form its loop.

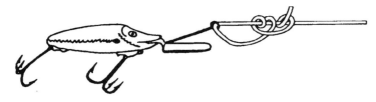

**Fig. 1** Pass the end of the line through the hook eye. Bring the line end forward and wrap it around the standing part of the line twice. Next bring the line end in front of the first wrap and wind it around the standing part of the line.

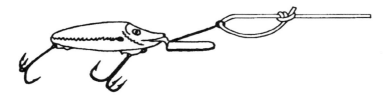

**Fig. 2** The finished Tautline Hitch.

**79**

## SLIDING OVERHEAD KNOT

It takes practice to tie this knot quickly, but the practice is worth it, since this is a good, strong knot, especially useful in knotting braided line or multi-strand wire. The trick to tying this knot is to be sure **both loops** slip back over the hook eye before pulling the knot tight.

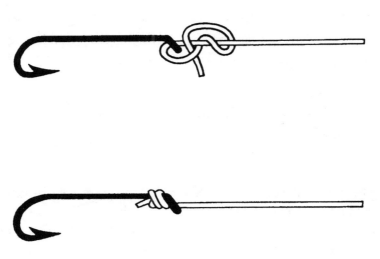

## LARK'S HEAD KNOT

The Lark's Head Knot is used extensively by natural bait fishermen, particularly bottomfishing marine anglers, for quickly securing hooks and sinkers. Some anglers also use this tie for attaching swivels and lures to line or leader. It can be tied and untied quickly, which is advantageous at times when it's necessary to change hooks or baits fast.

**Fig. 1** A loop is formed at the end of the line or leader, then the loop is passed through the hook, lure or swivel "eye."

**Fig. 2** The loop is then passed over the lure or swivel.

**Fig. 3** The knot is pulled tight.

## JANSIK SPECIAL KNOT

Unfortunately, very few anglers are familiar with the Jansik Special, yet it's a superb knot to use with monofilament line.

This knot isn't difficult to tie, and with a little practice it can be made in a few seconds.

To tie the Jansik Special, pass the end of the line through the hook eye twice. Then bring the line back around again, as though you were going to put the line through the hook eye three times. But instead, wrap the tag end of the fishing line three times around the monofilament loops. Pull the knot smoothly and carefully until tight. Moistening the knot with saliva helps tighten it.

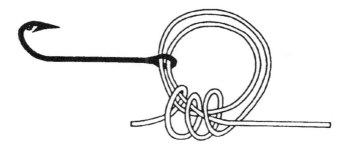

## CLINCH KNOT
### (Also called Half-Blood Knot and Stevedore Knot)

The Clinch Knot likely is the favorite and best-used knot among American anglers for tying a line to a hook or lure eye. It is a very secure, fast tie, and it can be made with heavy monofilament. When tying the Clinch Knot with heavy line, it's best to make only three or four turns rather than the standard five turns. This way the knot will tighten easier, yet will not lose much strength.

**Fig. 1** Pass the line end through the hook eye and pull about six inches of line through to tie the knot. Bring the end of the line back over the standing part, and wrap the end five times around the standing line. Next pass the line end back through the first loop.

**Fig. 2** Slowly pull on the standing part of the line and the line end, until the turns in the knot draw tightly against the hook eye.

**83**

## DAVE HAWK'S DROP-LOOP KNOT

Although this knot takes time to tie, even by an expert, it is a superb, firm connection. The Drop-Loop Knot is good because it allows a lure or fly to vibrate and wiggle freely, since the knot forms a loop rather than a tight tie against the lure.

This loop can be made with heavy mono, provided it's formed carefully, and tightened with pliers.

**Fig. 1** Tie a regular Overhand Knot in the line about five inches from its end and pull tight.

**Fig. 2** Pass the end of the line through the lure's connecting ring and bring it back parallel to the standing part of the line. Turn the line end down, forming a circle below the two parallel strands. Turn the line end around both parallel lines and through the circle twice, as shown.

**Fig. 3** Slowly draw the knot tight. Pull on the line and lure simultaneously so the knot slides down and jams tight against the Overhand Knot.

## PRIMA KNOT

This knot originated in Germany. Thread the leader through the hook eye, leaving at least six inches of leader with which to tie the knot. Next, form a loop with the end of the line and make a Double Overhand Knot, letting it hang below the hook. Then make a loop in the standing part of the leader, pass the loop through the opening of the Double Overhand Knot, and then loop it over the hook.

Slowly pull the Double Overhand Knot tight with the tag end of the leader, then pull the standing part of the line to tighten the knot behind the hook eye.

When this knot is tied properly it forms a secure connection, with the leader coming straight up and out from under the hook eye.

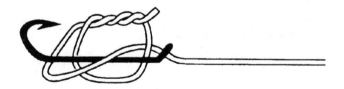

## RETURN KNOT

This knot was designed for tying monofilament leaders to a fly, lure or hook eye. Although comparatively few anglers are familiar with the Return Knot, it's very strong and not difficult to tie. This is a good knot for tying heavy-test nylon to lures, and especially bare hooks for bait fishermen.

**Fig. 1** Put the end of the line through the hook eye. Wrap the line around the hook, and hold the loop between your thumb and forefinger.

**Fig. 2** Make a second turn, like the first, and again hold the loop.

**Fig. 3** Pass the end of the line under both loops, and slowly pull on the standing part of the line. As the knot tightens be sure both loops are on the shank side of the hook eye.

**Fig. 4** The completed knot, tightened and trimmed.

## RETURN JAM KNOT

This knot is a variation of the Return Knot. And with practice an angler can make this knot in seconds.

The Return Jam Knot is easier to tie with light monofilament than with heavy test or braided line. The knot was designed for tying line to turned-up or turned-down hooks, and is a strong and dependable connection when properly tied.

**Fig. 1** Pass the leader through the hook eye and loosely wrap the line end around the hook shank.

**Fig. 2** Bring the line end around the standing part of the line.

**Fig. 3** Put the line end through the first loop made around the hook shank.

**Fig. 4** Make an Overhand Knot around the standing line behind the  hook eye.

**Fig. 5** The finished Return Jam Knot.

## DOUBLE EYE KNOT

The Double Eye Knot is a quick, secure tie that is most appreciated by natural bait fishermen. It can be used with all types of hooks, but is particularly good with ones having turned-down or turned-up "eyes."

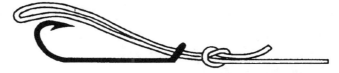

**Fig. 1** Double the line, forming a loop, then tie a simple Overhand Knot over the standing line. Pass the loop through the hook eye.

**Fig. 2** The loop now goes over the end of the hook, and is pulled up to the hook eye.

**Fig. 3** Take the "tag end" of the Overhand Knot and pass it under the loop, against the hook shank, and draw the knot tight.

**Fig. 4** The completed Double Eye Knot.

**90**

## FIGURE EIGHT KNOT

A fast knot to tie, the Figure Eight for that reason frequently is selected by anglers who want to change lures or flies quickly.  There are many fishing situations in which a nearly instant change of lures is vitally important.  This is particularly true when a fish that refuses one lure may be caught if the angler swiftly presents a different lure type or color to the fish.

The Figure Eight Knot holds best when tied with multi-strand wire or braided line, not so well with monofilament.

To tie a Figure Eight, put the end of the line through the hook eye, bring it back over the standing part of the line, and pass the line end back through the loop near the hook eye. Hold the hook or lure securely and pull the knot tight.

## QUICK SNELL KNOT

This is a good knot for snelling a hook fast. The Quick Snell Knot isn't as neat, nor does it hold as well, as a regular "snell." However, the Quick Snell is much easier to tie.

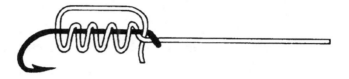

**Fig. 1** The hook eye is threaded with the line end. Then the line is wrapped four times around the hook shank. Next, the line end is put through the loop that's between the first wrap and the hook eye.

**Fig. 2** The tag end and the standing part of the line are tightened until the knot appears as illustrated.

## UNI-KNOT

This outstanding, versatile and durable knot was developed by renowned outdoor writer and angler Vic Dunaway. The Uni-Knot is more than a simple fishing knot, it is an entire knot-tying system. Here it's shown used to connect fishing line to a hook shank to create a fast snell that's ideal for natural bait fishing.

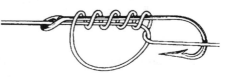

**Fig. 1** Run the fishing line through the hook eye, allowing 6-inches of line to make the knot. Form a loop with the tag line end as shown.

**Fig. 2** Make six turns with the tag end through the loop and around the hook shank.

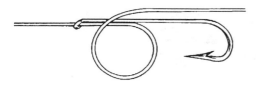

**Fig. 3** Pull the standing line tight and the knot will jam against the hook eye.

**93**

## DOUBLE SHEET BEND KNOT

The Double Sheet Bend Knot is much more versatile and stronger than the Single Sheet Bend. The Double Sheet Bend can be knotted fast, yet it makes an adequate connection for some angling situations, such as panfishing. Also, the Double Sheet Bend is a valuable knot for fishermen because it can be used to quickly form a "loop," which gives a lure or fly better action; or the knot can be drawn tight against the hook eye if such a tie is desired.

**Fig. 1** Put the line through the hook eye. Wrap the line end around the standing part of the line, and make an Overhand Knot. This will form a "slip knot."

**Fig. 2** Pull the knot tight. If desired, the Double Sheet Bend can be tightened above the hook eye to form a loop, or it can be jammed tight against the hook eye as shown.

## TWO-WRAP HANGMAN'S KNOT
### (Also called Figure Eight Knot)

This is a very valuable knot for any angler. The knot forms a loop so a lure or fly will have more action. It can be tied with either heavy or light monofilament.

The Two-Wrap Hangman's Knot is a sliding loop knot, so it can be tightened anywhere on the standing part of the fishing line, and a loop of any size can be made. In addition, when a fish strikes and is hooked, the knot will slide down and tighten against the hook eye. After the fish is landed, the knot can be slipped open and another loop formed.

**Fig. 1** Thread the line end through the hook eye, then make two wraps around the standing line back toward the hook eye. Keep the loops loose, holding them open with your fingers.

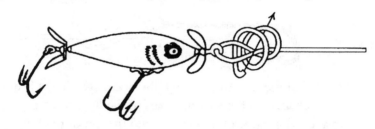

**Fig. 2** Push the line end back through the two loops, away from the hook or lure.

**Fig. 3** Hold the hook shank or lure with a pair of pliers, then slowly pull on the standing part of the line and tag end of the knot. When the knot is almost tight, it can be slid up or down the leader, forming the desired size loop. Then the knot is pulled completely tight.

## CADENAS KNOT
### (Sometimes called Double Hitch Jam Knot or Double Overhand Jam Knot)

This knot was originated in France, and is still used mainly by European anglers. The Cadenas Knot was designed for tying gut leaders to hooks, but it's also a quality knot for use with monofilament and braided line.

Some anglers use this knot instead of the Turle Knot because the Cadenas Knot makes a straight-line connection from the hook eye to the leader, and is particularly useful with hooks having turned-up or turned-down "eyes."

**Fig. 1** Put the line end through the hook eye. Then bring the line back around the standing part of the line, forming a circle. Now wind the line end twice around the top of the loop that was formed, as in making a Double Overhand Knot.

**Fig. 2** Slide the loop back over the hook eye, and slowly pull the knot snug.

## FAST SWIVEL KNOT

When tied properly, the Fast Swivel Knot is a satisfactory connection for many fishing situations. It is popular with anglers who use barrel swivels. Many fishermen who do a lot of trolling use this knot, and some anglers who use Carolina-rigged plastic worms also find the knot useful when rigging swivels above worms to prevent line twist.

Although this knot is primarily used with swivels, it also can be tied to a lure or hook. However, it isn't as secure as some other knots, such as the Improved Clinch Knot.

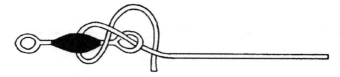

**Fig. 1** Thread the swivel eye with the line end. Wrap the line end around the swivel once, then under the standing part of the line and back over the swivel again.

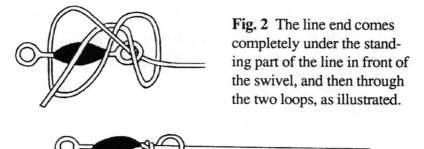

**Fig. 2** The line end comes completely under the standing part of the line in front of the swivel, and then through the two loops, as illustrated.

**Fig. 3** Both loops of the knot are tightened behind the swivel eye, and the knot is finished.

**97**

## CLINCH ON SHANK KNOT

The Clinch On Shank Knot is popular with bait fishermen. They like this knot because it's strong and permits a very direct pull from the center of the hook eye.

The most important part of tying this knot is to slowly pull and form the tie before tightening and trimming it.

## DOUBLE SNELL KNOTS

**(Commonly called Double Salmon Knots)**

Many salmon, steelhead and saltwater fishermen use two, three, four and more snelled hooks at the same time, each threaded with a natural bait. This is the best knot system to use when snelling more than one hook on a leader.

The Double Snelled Knot takes time to learn properly, but it's an extremely durable connection.

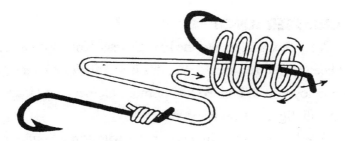

**Fig. 1** Snell the lower hook first, as usual. Then take the leader from the hook already snelled and loosely wind the end of the leader over the standing part of the leader and the shank of the second hook. Push the leader end through the loose loops.

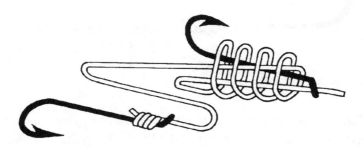

**Fig. 2** The leader end must be passed through all loops to make the knot secure. Then the tag end and the standing part of the leader are slowly tightened.

## EYE-CROSSER KNOT

Very few anglers use the Eye-Crosser Knot because it hasn't been publicized much. Yet this is an excellent knot when employed with braided line or monofilament, and it can be used with light or heavy test line.

The Eye-Crosser Knot is popular with some Southern bass fishermen who need a knot that's strong and won't pull out when heavy largemouths are hooked in brushy, snag-filled areas.

**Fig. 1** Pass the line end through the hook eye twice, leaving about eight inches of line to tie the knot. Bring the line end back parallel to the standing line, and pinch the two lines together with thumb and forefinger about two inches in front of the hook eye.

**Fig. 2** Wrap the line end around the two parallel strands three times.

**Fig. 3** Pull on the standing part of the line to bring the knot tight against the hook eye.

## OFFSHORE SWIVEL KNOT

The Offshore Swivel Knot is an excellent, strong, and unique knot that can be used not only for securing heavy-duty swivels to fishing line, but also for tying "doubled" monofilament line to a hook eye or to a lure's connecting ring.

The Swivel Knot is much easier to tie that it looks, and it can be made with even very heavy-test line. Moistening the knot wraps with saliva helps to tighten heavy, big-game fishing line.

One of the beauties of this knot for use with doubled line, is that if one line breaks during the course of a fish fight, the second line will hold, and the Offshore Swivel Knot will not unravel.

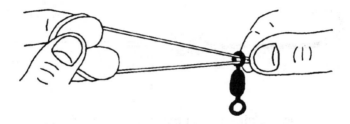

**Fig. 1** Make a doubled line—using a good knot such as the Bimini Twist or Spider Hitch—at the end of the fishing line. Now insert the doubled line through one "eye" of a heavy-duty swivel.

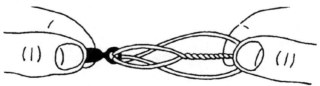

**Fig. 2** Bring the end of the doubled line back, and pinch it to the standing part of the doubled line.

**102**

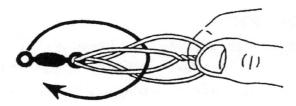

**Fig. 3** Pass the swivel through both loops of the doubled line.

**Fig. 4** Pass the swivel through both loops six or seven times, and the knot will look like this.

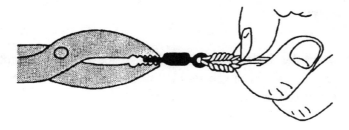

**Fig. 5** Hold the swivel with pliers, and begin tightening the knot by pulling on both standing parts of the doubled line with **even tension**. As the knot begins to tighten, push the wraps of the knot tight against the swivel to tighten it.

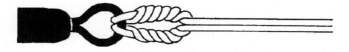

**Fig. 6** The completed Offshore Swivel Knot.

**103**

## CRAWFORD KNOT

The Crawford Knot often is overlooked by even skilled anglers, but it's a valuable tie that should be used more often. It's a very versatile knot for tying most types of hook, swivel and lure "eyes" to lines and leaders.

Despite its appearance, the Crawford Knot isn't difficult to tie, and it makes a solid, firm connection.

**Fig. 1** Insert the line through the hook eye, leaving about eight inches for tying the knot. Bring the line end back around the standing part of the line to form a loop.

**Fig. 2** Now bring the line end under the standing part of the line, and **over** the two parallel lines, as shown.

**104**

**Fig. 3** The knot has formed a "figure 8." Now bring the tag end of the line under the two parallel strands, then back over all three lines.

**Fig. 4** The knot is completed by tucking the tag end between the standing line and the front part of the loop. Pull the knot tight, slide it down and "jam" it against the hook eye and trim.

## TWO CIRCLE TURLE KNOT

This is one of the most-used knots in Europe for tying a hook or fly to monofilament. As with all variations of the Turle Knot, the Two Circle Turle Knot is normally used to tie hooks—especially flies—with turned-up or turned-down eyes to leaders.

Most fishermen believe that the Turle Knot was invented by a Major Turle of England. However, as the Major himself reported, he didn't design the many different Turle Knots, but rather learned them from his numerous fishing companions.

**Fig. 1** Push the leader end through the hook eye, and slide the hook up the leader out of the way. Form a circle with the leader about six inches from the leader's end.

**Fig. 2** Make a second loop identical to the first, and overlay the two loops.

**Fig. 3** Now tie an Overhand Knot over the two loops, as illustrated, and tighten it.

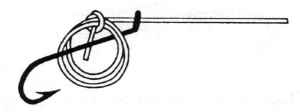

**Fig. 4** Put the hook, lure or fly through the two loops.

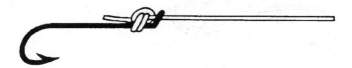

**Fig. 5** Pull on the leader end and its standing part until the knot tightens behind the hook eye. The trimmed, finished knot is shown.

**107**

## BRUBAKER KNOT

This is an excellent knot for use with all monofilament fishing lines, but especially lines testing 50-pounds and more. This knot is a favorite of world-champion caster and angler Bruce Brubaker, who considers it an exceptional tie for heavy monofilament when chasing stout gamefish such as tarpon and sharks.

**Fig. 1** Insert the line end through the hook eye, then wrap the tag end around the standing line as shown.

**Fig. 2** Wrap the line end three times around the standing line.

**108**

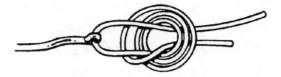

**Fig. 3** Now put the line end back through the open line loops.

**Fig. 4** Pull the line ends to tighten the knot.

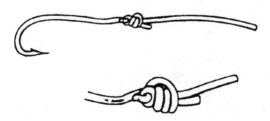

**Fig. 5** Slide the knot down to the hook eye, which is most easily done if the knot is moistened with saliva.

## HOMER'S KNOT

Homer Circle, angling editor of Sports Afield for many years, spent countless hours devising this knot. Extensive testing by Circle showed this knot to be one of the strongest available for securing fishing line to a hook eye or swivel ring. The knot is especially useful for lines testing under 20-pounds.

**Fig. 1** Run the line end through the hook eye, leaving about six inches of line to tie the knot. Then tie an Overhand Knot around the standing line with the tag end, as shown.

**Fig. 2** Make three turns with the line tag end around the standing line, **away** from the hook eye and overhand knot.

**Fig. 3** Bend the tag line end around the standing line, and hold the loop with your thumb and forefinger. Now make three more turns with the line end back **toward** the hook, then run the end through the overhand knot.

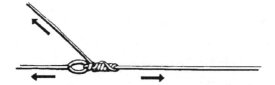

**Fig. 4** Pull on the line tag end, standing line, and hook to tighten the knot. Then trim the tag end close.

*Ultralight trout fishing is demanding sport, with no margin for error for the angler or his tackle.*

## WORLD'S FAIR KNOT

This knot was created by Gary Martin of Lafayette, Indiana and was first demonstrated by him at the Knoxville 1982 World's Fair, hence its name.

It's an excellent, easy-to-tie, all-purpose knot for securing fishing line to any connecting ring.

**Fig. 1** Double a 6-inch length of line and pass the loop through the eye.

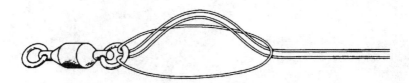

**Fig. 2** Bring the loop back next to the doubled line and grasp the doubled line through the loop.

**112**

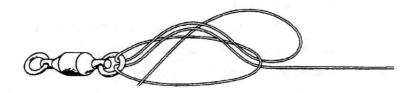

**Fig. 3** Put the tag end through the new loop formed by the double line.

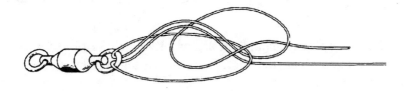

**Fig. 4** Bring the tag end back through the new loop created by step 3.

**Fig. 5** Pull the tag end snug, and slide the knot tight to the connecting ring. Trim tag end.

**113**

## THE RAPALA KNOT

This loop knot was designed to allow the light Rapala lure to have the utmost action during the retrieve. This non-slip loop knot does not interfere with the slight wobbles and wiggles the fish-catching Rapala plug has. Of course, this loop knot works well with other lures, and is very strong when tied correctly.

**Fig. 1** Tie an overhand knot, leaving five inches of line with which to complete the knot, then pass the tag end through the lure's line-tie ring.

**Fig. 2** Pass the tag end back through the overhand knot.

**Fig. 3** Wind the tag end three times around the standing part of the line.

**114**

**Fig. 4** Pass the tag end back through the overhand knot.

**Fig. 5** Now thread the tag end through the loop formed.

**Fig. 6** Moisten the knot, pull it tight, and trim closely.

## WHIP FINISH HOOK SNELL

This is one of the fastest and easiest ways to snell a hook, and it can be made with very heavy test line. It's simply a whip-finish knot, popular with fly tiers and rod makers. It's every bit as secure as other snell knots, and is popular with natural bait fishermen.

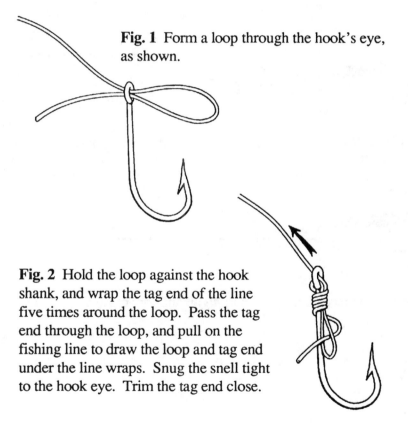

**Fig. 1** Form a loop through the hook's eye, as shown.

**Fig. 2** Hold the loop against the hook shank, and wrap the tag end of the line five times around the loop. Pass the tag end through the loop, and pull on the fishing line to draw the loop and tag end under the line wraps. Snug the snell tight to the hook eye. Trim the tag end close.

# Loops and Specialty Knots

There are many line connections that satisfy special fishing needs. But most of this chapter is dedicated to forming and tying various kinds of loops. Loops are essential, in one form or another, in almost all types of fishing.

For example, one of the most famous and valued loops included in this chapter is the Bimini Twist. The Bimini is used to form a doubled line, and is of vital importance when severe line end wear is likely. But while many light-tackle marine anglers use the Bimini, most freshwater anglers do not—though they should. The Bimini has the reputation of being a very difficult knot to tie. But with just a bit of practice it's a simple knot that's essential to a quality terminal tackle system in many types of angling.

Loops like the Bimini, Spider Hitch, Surgeon's Loop and others can make your fishing easier, more successful and more fun.

### ARBOR KNOT

This is the quickest, easiest way of tying monofilament or braided line to any type reel.

First pass the line around the reel spool and tie a simple Overhand Knot. Now tie another Overhand Knot with the short end of the line around the standing part of the line to bring both of the Overhand Knots together. Trim the short end of the knot, then wind the line onto the reel.

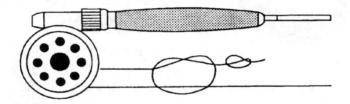

## END LOOP KNOT

This loop knot is simple to tie, and can be made in seconds.

The End Loop works well with monofilament and braided line. Its primary purpose is to form a doubled line for the basis of a leader system.

**Fig. 1** Double the end of the line, leaving about six inches of doubled line with which to tie the knot.

**Fig. 2** Wind the doubled line back over itself five times.

**Fig. 3** Take the end of the doubled line and pass it through the first loop. Now tighten the knot by pulling on the standing line and the tag end, as well as on the doubled line.

**Fig. 4** The finished End Loop.

## BIMINI TWIST
### (Also called 20-Times Around Knot, Rollover Knot, and the100 Percent Knot)

Although some knots perform almost equally as well as the Bimini and are easier to tie (such as the Spider Hitch), many veteran anglers (especially saltwater fishermen) still prefer the Bimini Twist for making a doubled line that will have 100 percent knot strength. The Bimini is a mainstay of light-tackle anglers for building a leader system foundation. It is often the knot that connects the main fishing line to shock tippets, as well as forming "double back" line in big game trolling.

While the Bimini has a reputation as being one of the most difficult of all knots to tie, it isn't that tough to make if the steps shown here are followed carefully. Tying the Bimini correctly, however, does take more practice than most other knots, but with a little diligence, anyone can learn to make this knot in a short time.

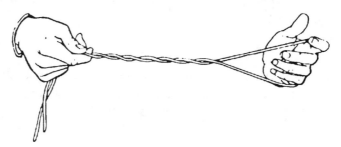

**Fig. 1** This step determines how large a loop will be created with the Bimini Twist. For most light tackle situations, 6- to 12-feet of line is doubled, creating a "loop" 3- to 6-feet in size. Form a loop in one hand while holding the line end and

standing part together firmly in the other hand. Then twist the loop 20 times.

**Fig. 2** Now fit the loop over a stationary, non-abrasive object, like a boat cleat, or even your foot.

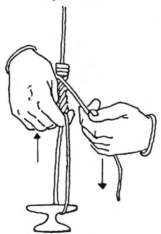

**Fig. 3** This is the most critical part of the knot, and the step most beginners find difficult. While pulling on the standing part of the line, "open" and increase the size of the loop by inserting your index finger in the loop and pulling the knot wraps **away** from the stationary object. As the knot wraps "gather" or jam tightly—while keeping constant pressure to

**121**

maintain the open loop—pull the tag end of the line **back toward the loop.** This will cause the tight, jammed line wraps to double over themselves. By keeping **constant pressure** on the loop, standing line, and tag end, it's accomplished with some practice.

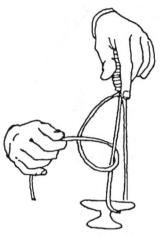

**Fig. 4** Maintain tension on the loop, standing line, and knot wraps, until you put a Half-Hitch in one side of the loop.

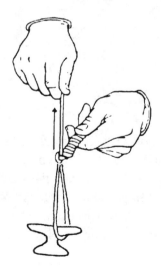

**Fig. 5** Tightening the Half-Hitch secures the Bimini's wraps.

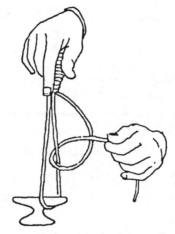

**Fig. 6** Put another Half-Hitch on the other side of the loop to "lock" the Bimini's wraps in place.

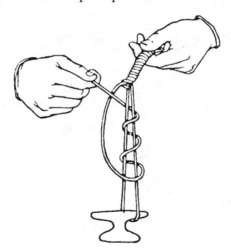

**Fig. 7** Wind the tag end of the knot three to five times around the large loop, then push the line end back through the small loop just made and tighten.

**123**

**Fig. 8** The completed Bimini Twist should look like this, with the loop made to any size desired.

## LEADER LOOP KNOT

The Leader Loop Knot is a good, strong knot for tying a loop in a line to which a leader may be attached. It can be tied fast, but is best made with stiff monofilament, braided line or fly line.

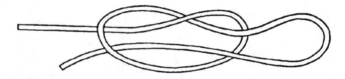

**Fig. 1** Tie a loose Overhand Knot about six inches from the end of the line. Pass the end of the line through the center of the Overhand Knot.

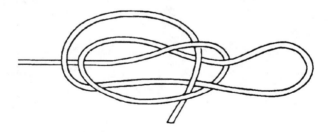

**Fig. 2** The end of the line is then brought around the Overhand Knot and passed through the two openings of the knot.

**124**

**Fig. 3** The finished Leader Loop Knot after the tag end has been trimmed.

*The Bimini Twist is a standard terminal tackle knot when high-leaping action from sailfish is on tap.*

**125**

## PERMANENT LOOP SPLICE IN DACRON

This loop can be made in Dacron line very quickly, because this type of braided line has a hollow core. Dacron is used often by fly-rodders for backing line, and by trollers (especially big game marine anglers) because it has limited stretch. This splice is extremely strong, and valuable to anglers because it eliminates the need for a bulky knot. Also, this loop won't pull out because the line end is pushed through the standing part of the line for **at least** eight inches.

Because a knot isn't used to make this tie, it goes through rod guides very smoothly. For that reason, some fly fishermen prefer it over using knots, and connect backing lines to fly lines with interconnecting loops.

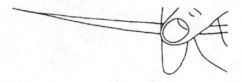

**Fig. 1** Bend a piece of light, thin wire into a sharp "V."

**Fig. 2** Insert the pointed end of the wire "V" into the center of the Dacron line. Where you insert the wire will determine the size of the loop formed.

**126**

**Fig. 3** Push the wire through and out of the Dacron line, about 8- to 10-inches from where the wire was inserted.

**Fig. 4** Secure the end of the Dacron line in the wire loop.

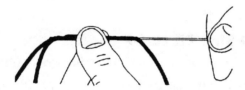

**Fig. 5** Withdraw the wire "V" from the Dacron, which in turn will pull the Dacron line end through the center of the standing part of the line.

**Fig. 6** The completed Dacron loop.

**127**

## SPLIT-SHOT SINKER LOOP

This loop eliminates tying and untying knots to a lure or hook. The line is doubled, and a split-shot sinker (or two) is clamped around the two lines to form a loop. The loop is threaded through the hook eye and then slipped over the lure or hook, as shown, which secures the tie.

This loop is not recommended for large fish. But it's an adequate, quick tie for panfish.

SPLIT-SHOT
SINKER

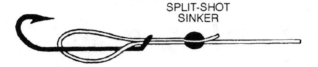

## TWO-RING SINKER LOOP

This method of attaching a two-ring sinker often is used by anglers fishing natural baits for panfish. It's beneficial to those anglers because the sinker can be put on or removed in seconds, or easily adjusted anywhere on the fishing line.

To form the loop, simply double the line and insert it through both of the sinker's rings. Then push the line end through the loop, as illustrated, and pull to tighten.

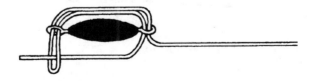

**128**

## SINGLE OVERHAND LOOP KNOT
**(Also called Overhand Eye Knot and Common Loop Knot)**

This is the easiest knot for making a loop in the end of a length of line. Simply double the line, and make an Overhand Knot. Other loop knots are stronger, but for most light fishing it's adequate.

## SURGEON'S LOOP
**(Also called Double Overhand Knot, Two-Fold Water Knot, Two-Fold Blood Knot, Line Knot and Double Surgeon's Loop)**

This is one of the best end loop knots available to anglers. It's extremely strong, and can be made with virtually any pound test line. It's simply a double overhand knot, but it resists cutting itself. Be sure to tighten the knot well before using it.

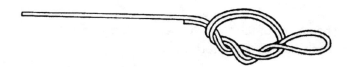

## DROPPER LOOP
### (Also called Blood Dropper Loop)

The Dropper Loop is very popular with some anglers who fish more than one lure or bait simultaneously. The loop can be tied quickly and it's secure. Once the loop is tied, another leader with a lure attached may be fastened to the loop.

This is a popular knot for bottom fishermen, especially catfish anglers and snapper/grouper fishermen, who use multiple baits off a single leader. The Dropper Loop also can be used to position a sinker weight on a leader.

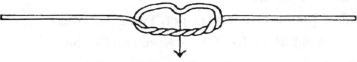

**Fig. 1** Make a "circle" in the line where you want to position the dropper. The two lines that form the circle are "pinched" together, then the circle is twisted five times around the two crossed lines. Done correctly, the circle will appear as in the illustration.

**Fig. 2** The center of the twisted lines is opened, and the "circle" is pushed through, forming a "loop."

**Fig. 3** Now the two standing parts of the line are drawn tight. A finger, hook or pencil should be placed in the loop to prevent it from pulling out while tightening.

**Fig. 4** The finished Dropper Loop.

*Huge salmon tax an angler's skills to the maximum, and there is no room for line or knot-tying errors.*

**131**

## PERFECTION LOOP
### (Fishermen's Loop, Compound Knot)

The Perfection Loop is one of the strongest loop knots known.  But many anglers have forsaken it because they believe it's too difficult to tie.  However, the following method of tying the Perfection Loop is easy and very fast.

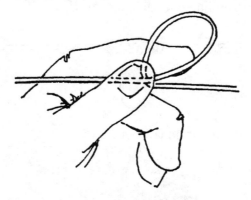

**Fig. 1** Form a "circle" about eight inches from the line end and "pinch" it tightly, as shown.

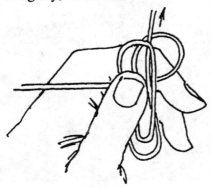

**Fig. 2** This step seems a little tricky, but it's quite simple. While holding the "circle" between your thumb and forefin-

ger, take the line end and wrap it **over** your thumbnail then back **under** the circle.

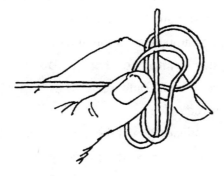

**Fig. 3** Now, make a second wrap in front of the first wrap, and hold it **under** your thumb.

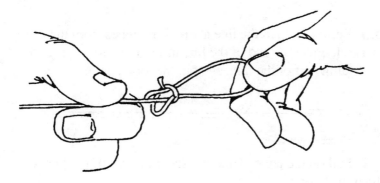

**Fig. 4** Finally, slip the **first wrap** off your thumbnail, and pull it through the open "circle. This first "wrap" forms the Perfection Loop as the knot is drawn tight. Trim tag end close.

## BOWLINE KNOT

Although the Bowline is normally considered a boating knot, it's also valuable to anglers.

A Bowline can be used to put a loop in the end of a line so a leader may be attached. Too, the Bowline is excellent for tying a "loop knot" onto a lure so it "swims" more freely when retrieved.

The major advantages of the Bowline are that it can be tied in seconds, it's extremely strong, and won't slip.

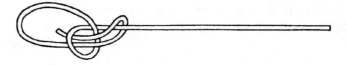

**Fig. 1** Form a loop in the line about four inches from the line's end. Push the end of the line through the loop, around the standing part of the line, and out the loop again.

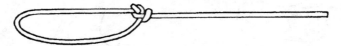

**Fig. 2** Pull on the tag end and the standing part of the line to tighten the knot.

**134**

## CROTCH SPLICE

Although this splice takes time, it's very secure for joining braided lines and also for splicing two fly lines.

**Fig. 1** Use a pin or needle to fray the ends of the two lines. Fray about one inch of each line.

**Fig. 2** Fork the frayed ends of both lines as shown. Then push the two "crotches" of each frayed end together.

**Fig. 3** Wind the splice tightly with heavy nylon thread and tie off. Cut the loose ends of the protruding fibers.

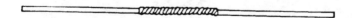

**Fig. 4** Continue wrapping the splice with nylon thread until it looks like this. Coat splices with lacquer or Pliobond cement.

**135**

## SPIDER HITCH KNOT

Many anglers use the Spider Hitch instead of the
Bimini Twist when they want a knot that will double their line.
The Spider Hitch can be quickly tied, and it has superb knot
strength.

The Spider Hitch can be tied effortlessly—with either
monofilament or braided lines—to form a double line having
twice the strength of a single strand.  It also works well with
heavy monofilament.

**Fig. 1** Double the line, then put a small reverse loop in it.

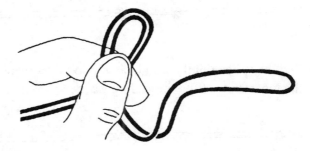

**Fig. 2** Hold the reverse loop with thumb and forefinger.

**136**

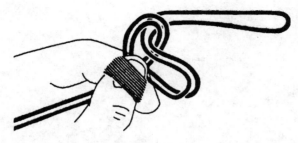

**Fig. 3** Wrap the doubled line five times around the thumb and the reverse loop.

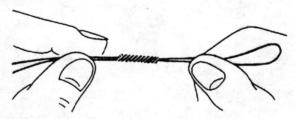

**Fig. 4** Slowly pull the large loop so the line unwinds off the thumb. To make a small, properly-formed knot, it's important to pull all four lines of the connection firmly and evenly while tightening.

*Giant steelhead, like this massive 26-pounder from British Columbia's Babine River, test a fly fisherman's knots like few fish in freshwater.*

# 5  Knots For Fly Fishing

The nature of fly fishing requires that special knots be used to connect leader sections, tippets, fly lines to leaders, and fly lines to backing. The knots in this chapter are of special use to fly fishermen, though other anglers may find these knots valuable, too.

By having knots of practical use for fly fishermen grouped here in a single chapter, a fly angler can immediately locate and learn to tie knots that fill his specific needs.

## FLY LINE LOOP
**(Method One)**

Some fly-rodders shy away from fly line loops because they're too bulky. However, when made properly, this fly line loop is sleek, strong, and very useful in quickly changing fly lines.

**Fig. 1** Dip about three inches of the fly line in nail-polish remover and scrape off the loosened fly line coating.

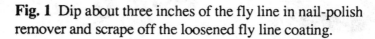

**Fig. 2** Fold the fly line "core" back, forming a loop.

**Fig. 3** Bind the two fly line cores tightly together with size 00 nylon thread. Coat the thread with lacquer or rubber cement like Pliobond.

## FLY LINE LOOP
**(Method Two)**

**Fig. 1** Use nail-polish remover to take off one-inch of finish from the end of the fly line, revealing its core.

**Fig. 2** Take a three-inch piece of braided line, 15- to 25-pound test, and double it over the "cleaned" fly line.

**Fig. 3** Tightly wrap over the two ends of bait-casting line and fly line core with size OO nylon thread. Coat the wraps with lacquer or Pliobond.

## DOUBLE NAIL-KNOT LOOP

This loop can be made with any line, but it's most often used by fly fishermen, especially those using monofilament fly lines that have a smooth, slick-surface coating.

To make the loop, double back the line to form the desired size loop. Then, using a couple lengths of light monofilament line, tie two Fast Nail Knots about 1/4-inch apart around both strands of the loop. The Fast Nail Knots can be coated with Pliobond or other rubber-based cement, which aids the connection in passing through rod guides.

## TURLE KNOT

This is an old, reliable knot that's particularly popular with fly fishermen. The Turle Knot is quick and simple to tie. Also, it's extremely valuable to fly-rodders because it's designed specifically for tying on hooks with turned-up or turned-down eyes.

Because the leader passes through the hook eye, in-line with the shank, when you strike fish the hook moves in a direct line. That helps considerably in sinking the barb.

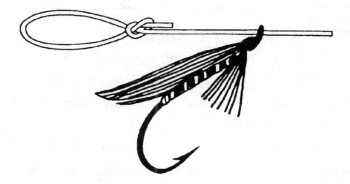

**Fig. 1** The line end goes through the hook eye, and a loop is formed in the line. A simple Overhand Knot is tied around the standing part of the line.

**Fig. 2** The loop is enlarged enough so that the fly passes through.

**Fig. 3** With the loop tight behind the hook eye, the knot is pulled tight against the neck of the fly.

**Fig. 4** The leader is drawn tight through the hook eye, and the line end is trimmed close to the knot.

**143**

## DOUBLE TURLE KNOT

This is merely a standard Turle Knot carried one step farther. Instead of making a single wrap with the Overhand Knot, as when tying the standard Turle Knot, two wraps are made with the line end around the standing part of the line before passing the hook back through the loop.

The regular Turle Knot originally was designed for tying gut leaders to hooks with turned-up or turned-down eyes. The Double Turle Knot, however, was created for use with nylon monofilament lines. It is stronger and more dependable than the Turle Knot.

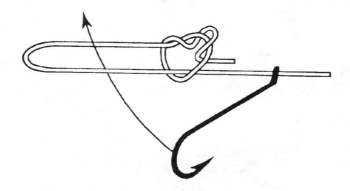

## WYSS TURLE KNOT

This is an ordinary Turle Knot, with an extra step before the knot is pulled tight. Many fishermen use the Wyss Turle Knot rather than the regular Turle Knot because the Wyss Turle Knot is less likely to slip and break from pressure exerted by strong fish.

**144**

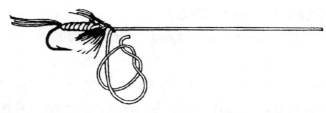

**Fig. 1** Thread the leader through the hook eye. Bring the end of the leader back and tie an Overhand Knot around the standing part of the leader.

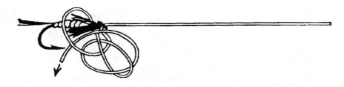

**Fig. 2** Slip the loop formed by the Overhand Knot over the hook shank, and bring the end of the leader through the loop that's now around the hook shank.

**Fig. 3** Hold the tag end of the leader against the hook shank, and slowly pull on the standing part of the leader to tighten the knot around the fly's head behind the hook eye.

## SPECIALIST FLY KNOT

This innovative version of the Clinch Knot was first made popular by the Berkley Tackle Company, and has since proven to be a useful and very secure knot. While the Specialist Knot primarily is used by fly anglers, the knot also is a good one for anglers casting jigs, some plugs and even single hooks for use with plastic worms.

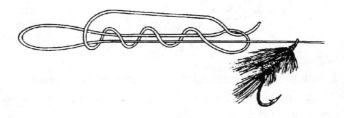

**Fig. 1** Insert the leader end through the fly's hook eye and allow about 8-inches of line to tie the knot. Form an oval loop with the line end and standing part of the leader. While holding each end of the loop, wrap the leader end four times around the loop. Then bring the leader end through the loop end closest to the fly's hook eye.

**146**

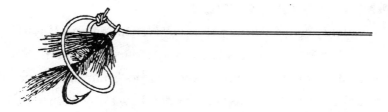

**Fig. 2** Pull the knot tight, then position the resulting loop around the fly's hook bend so the loop will tighten around the hook-eye ring.

**Fig. 3** Pull the leader tight, trim the knot close.

## PORTLAND CREEK HITCH
### (Commonly called Riffling Hitch or Newfoundland Hitch)

The Portland Creek Hitch is used often by stream salmon and trout fly fishermen who want to "skim" a fly over the surface. This knot makes the leader draw away from the head of the fly at a 45-degree angle, causing the fly to "swim" and make a "V" wake on the surface. Such action can be irresistible to salmon and trout.

When a heavy fish strikes the fly, the "hitch" usually slips off the fly's head without knotting the leader.

Tying this knot properly is very important in determining the way the fly "works" in water. Some European salmon guides spend much time tying and re-tying the Portland Creek Hitch, as they inspect the fly in the water to see that it has the correct action before going fishing.

The Portland Creek Hitch can be used with many streamers, "hopper" imitations and some dry flies. The flies look very alive when skipped or skimmed across the surface with the Hitch, which draws strikes from cautious, clear-water fish. Western trout are especially vulnerable to "hopper" patterns when the Portland Hitch is employed.

**Fig. 1** Tie the leader to the fly with a Turle Knot, then tie a Half-Hitch in the leader and pull it over the fly's head.

**Fig. 2** Tighten the Half-Hitch behind the fly's head so the leader comes away at the bottom or side.

## NAIL KNOT
### (Also called Tube Knot)

This knot is used to join a large diameter line to a small diameter line, as when tying a shock tippet to a leader, or fly line to backing line. It is an **extremely** good knot that won't pull out and resists fraying, especially if coated with a rubber-type cement. It is not a bulky knot and will readily go through rod guides when tied and trimmed correctly. Although a nail was originally used in tying this famous knot, many modern anglers use a small plastic tube, ice pike, piece of coat hanger, soda straw, straightened paper clip, or even an air-pump needle. It doesn't matter what "tool" is used, so long as its surface is smooth so the monofilament slides off the tool easily.

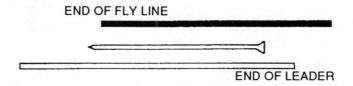

**Fig. 1** Position the fly line and leader with the nail between, as shown.

**Fig. 2** Wrap the leader toward the fly line end, making five tight turns. Pass the end back through the center of the loops.

**150**

**Fig. 3** This is how the knot should look, nail still in place.

**Fig. 4** Pull on both leader ends, and slowly withdraw the nail.

**Fig. 5** Once the nail is removed, pull tightly on all four line strands protruding from the knot.

**Fig. 6** The finished knot, with tag ends trimmed.

**151**

## NAIL KNOT USING HOOK

This is a very practical and easy way to tie a Nail Knot. It can "save the day" for those anglers who forget to bring tubes or other "tools" to tie Nail Knots while fishing.

The trick in tying this knot is to keep the leader loops very loose until the hook eye and leader end are pulled through the loops. The knot is then pulled tight and the leader end trimmed close. It is most easily formed and made with a "needle-eye" hook, as such a hook will smoothly pull through the wraps of the Nail Knot.

LEADER · FLY LINE

## NAIL KNOT USING LINE-LOOP

This an ordinary Nail Knot but no nail or tube is needed to tie it. This method of tying a Nail Knot is useful when nails, tubes, etc., are not available.

**Fig. 1** Cut a short piece of line, double it over and lay alongside the fly line. Make six turns with leader end, and bring through the loop in the short piece of line.

**152**

**Fig. 2** Pull short line through loops of knot, which will bring leader end with it, as shown.

**Fig. 3** Pull tightly on both ends of leader to tighten knot.

**Fig. 4** Trim short ends of the fly line, leader.

*When fishing for huge, strong fish, such as this amberjack held by the author's father Tom McNally, fly-rodders must be certain their fly line-backing line connection is strong and small—so it will zip through rod guides with ease.*

**153**

## FAST NAIL KNOT
### (Also called Speed Nail Knot and 20-Second Nail Knot)

Many anglers do not use the Nail Knot because tying it often is difficult and time consuming. However, the Fast Nail Knot is one of the easiest, quickest and most secure knots for joining two lines of similar diameters.

No special tool is needed to tie this knot. A nail, paper clip, match stick, toothpick, or any other stiff, small diameter object may be used. A slick-surface item like a nail or paper clip is best, as the knot "wraps" after it's been fully formed slip off best for final tightening.

This knot is much like "Snelling a Hook," so if you practice "snelling," tying the Fast Nail Knot will be much easier.

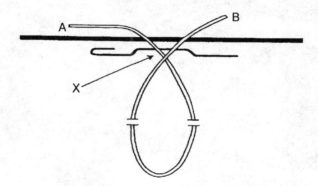

**Fig. 1** Hold a paper clip (or similar rigid item) parallel to the fly line. Form a loop with the nylon monofilament, and lay it over the fly line and paper clip. "A" is the leader butt, "B" is the leader point or tip. All components are held at point "X" with the thumb and forefinger of the left hand.

**154**

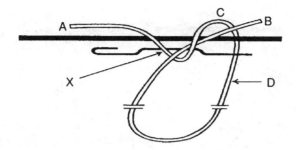

**Fig. 2** Continue holding all components at "X," and with the right hand holding the mono leader at about "D" begin rolling the monofilament line over itself at "C." The mono is looped over itself, the fly line, and the paper clip.

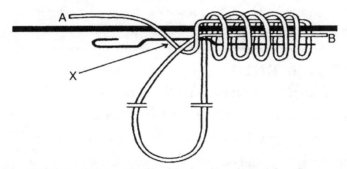

**Fig. 3** Still holding at "X" with the thumb and forefinger, wrap the mono around itself, the fly line, and the clip about six times.

**Fig. 4** Holding firmly at "X," pull the mono end "B" through on the right side of the knot until the knot tightens. Leader end "B" will lengthen as the mono (or leader) is pulled through the Nail Knot.

**155**

**Fig. 5** Now the paper clip is withdrawn from the knot, and the knot is tightened by pulling on both "A" and "B" ends of the monofilament.

**Fig. 6** The completed Fast Nail Knot looks like this after it has been trimmed and tightened.

## DOUBLE NAIL KNOT

This knot is important to fly fishermen because it's less bulky and easier to form than a Blood Knot when tying leaders of heavy monofilament. As with a Blood Knot, the two leader strands should be of nearly equal diameter for the knot to hold well.

**Fig. 1** Wrap one leader strand four times around the other and around the nail, then pass the first leader end back through the loops, as illustrated.

**156**

**Fig. 2** Remove the nail, and pull the first knot partially tight.

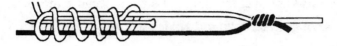

**Fig. 3** Tie the second knot the same way, as shown. Again withdraw the nail, and tighten the knot as done before.

**Fig. 4** Push both knots together to "jam," then tighten.

## OFFSET NAIL KNOT

Although this is an elaborate and somewhat complex knot to tie, it's one of the best for joining two strands of monofilament having different diameters. Some anglers prefer this knot over the Surgeon's Knot because the Offset Nail Knot goes through rod guides so easily.

**Fig. 1** Wind the heavy line twice around the lighter line and the nail. Then push the heavy line end back through the center, as illustrated. Remove the nail and partially tighten the knot.

**Fig. 2** Wrap the lighter test line eight times around the heavier test line and the nail, then push the end of the lighter test line back through the loops.

**Fig. 3** Remove the nail and slowly pull all four ends tight.

**Fig. 4** This is how the finished knot looks.

**158**

*When giant pike are the target, fly-rodders must be able to tie heavy shock tippets to flies with knots such as the Buffer Loop.*

**159**

## MODIFIED NAIL KNOT

Although this type Nail Knot can be used to join almost any kind of line, it was originally designed for connecting lead-core trolling line to monofilament. Fly-rodders also use the Modified Nail Knot for joining lead-core fly lines to leaders and backing. It can be employed for connecting coated braided wire to leaders.

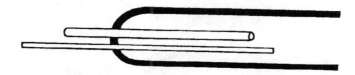

**Fig. 1** Lay two lines next to each other, as shown, alongside a plastic or metal tube, like tying a standard Nail Knot.

**Fig. 2** Wind one line around the tube and the second line.

**Fig. 3** After three wraps with the first line, take both lines and wind them once around the tube.

**Fig. 4** Continue wrapping with the first line.

**Fig. 5** Next pass the first line back through the tube, pull the lines snug, slip the tube out, and tighten.

**Fig. 6** This is how the completed knot looks.

## VARIATION OF THE NAIL KNOT

This quick and easy knot is best used when tying a heavy leader butt to a fly line. Because there are only a few wraps, some anglers feel this knot is easier to tie than a conventional Nail Knot. However, some other Nail Knots, such as the Fast Nail Knot, are even easier to tie than this one, and are stronger. Still, this Variation Of The Nail Knot is useful to anglers who have difficulty tying other knots.

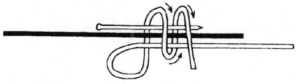

**Fig. 1** No tying is done with the fly line. Hold the nail parallel to the fly line and form a loop with the leader butt.

**Fig. 2** Hold loop below fly line, wrap leader's butt end twice around the fly line, nail and standing part of leader.

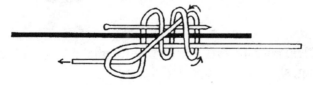

**Fig. 3** Put butt end through last wrap and first loop, as shown.

**Fig. 4** Push all the wraps tightly together with thumb nail, and withdraw the nail slowly.

**162**

**Fig. 5** Pull all line ends, then trim.

## NEEDLE NAIL KNOT

This is an excellent knot for joining a leader to a fly line. The knot takes more time than a conventional Nail Knot, but some anglers believe their fly leaders lay straighter because this knot is used.

LEADER    NEEDLE    FLY LINE

**Fig. 1** Push the needle through the blunt end of the fly line and out again about 1/4-inch from the end. Put the end of the leader through the needle eye, and pull the needle through the fly line, which will bring the nylon leader after it.

**Fig. 2** Now tie a conventional Nail Knot, but use the needle instead of a nail. Make four to six wraps around the needle, then put the end of the leader through the needle eye.

**Fig. 3** Now pull the needle through the knot, and the leader will follow.

**Fig. 4** After the short leader end is trimmed, the finished knot looks like this.

**163**

## NEEDLE KNOT

This is a faster, more easily tied knot than the Needle Nail Knot.  Although it isn't as secure a tie as the Needle Nail Knot, this version of the Needle Knot is a good connection for light, freshwater fly fishing.

Some fly-rodders choose this knot because the leader butt comes directly from the center of the fly line.  They believe that causes the fly leader to lie straighter on the water than with some other knots.

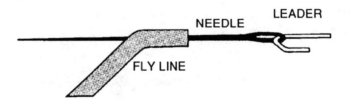

**Fig. 1** Thread the leader butt through the "eye" of the needle. Push the needle through the center of the fly line, then out about one-half inch from the line end.

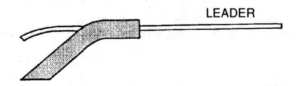

**Fig. 2** This is how the knot should look thus far.

**164**

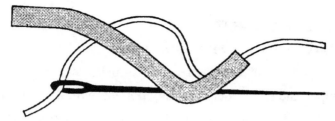

**Fig. 3** Push the needle completely through the fly line a second time, one inch above the point where the needle passed through the line initially. Then insert the needle a third time—into and out of the fly line—as illustrated.

**Fig. 4** At this stage the knot should look like this.

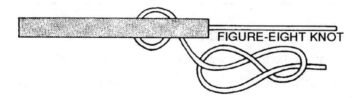

FIGURE-EIGHT KNOT

**Fig. 5** Tie a Figure Eight Knot in the end of the leader butt.

**Fig. 6** Pull on the standing part of the leader to draw the Needle Knot tight.

**165**

## ANGLER'S KNOT
### (Also called Single Fishermen's Knot)

This is an excellent, quick-to-make knot for tying a dropper line to a leader. It's very popular with fly fishermen, but it's also useful for bait-casters and spin fishermen who want to fish two or more lures at the same time. The Angler's Knot is simple to tie—just make two Overhand Knots, each around the standing part of the other line.

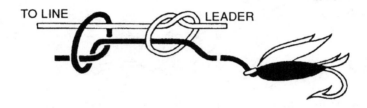

## DROPPER SNELL KNOT

This is the fastest way to connect the line from a snelled fly to a leader for fly fishing. The Dropper Snell isn't as good as some other knots for attaching droppers, such as the Extension Blood Knot. But the Dropper Snell is adequate for most light, freshwater fishing.

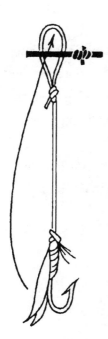

**Fig. 1** Hold the loop of the dropper line at a right angle to the leader and bring the fly up through the loop in the dropper line.

**Fig. 2** Pull on the dropper fly to tighten the knot. It's best to tie the Dropper Snell Knot just above a knot in the main leader to keep the Snell Knot from "sliding" down the leader.

**167**

## BUFFER LOOP KNOT

The Buffer Loop is one of the better knots for attaching a fly to a heavy monofilament "shock tippet." The knot is fast and simple to tie, and is used often by fly-rodders pursuing large or toothy gamefish. The Buffer Loop forms a loop through the "eye" of a fly, so the fly has a lifelike action when retrieved.

This knot should be used only with monofilament leaders that are so thick that it isn't practical to use an Improved Clinch Knot.

**Fig. 1** Tie an Overhand Knot about six inches from the end of the line, then pass the line through the fly's hook eye.

**Fig. 2** Put the line end through the open Overhand Knot and tie a Half-Hitch with the line end onto the standing part of the line.

**168**

**Fig. 3** Slide the Overhand Knot either up or down the standing part of the line. This will determine the size of the loop the knot will form. Slowly pull the line's end and its standing part to tighten the knot.

**Fig. 4** Trim the knot, leaving a tag end about 1/8-inch long.

## IMPROVED CLINCH KNOT
### (Also called Pandre Knot or Jam Knot With An Extra Tuck)

The Improved Clinch Knot is considered by veteran fly fishermen to be among the strongest knots for attaching flies to leaders ranging from light to medium-heavy.

The Improved Clinch Knot can be tied very quickly, even in poor light, and it forms only a small, straight connection at the hook eye.

When using heavy leader tippets of 40-pound test or more, it isn't always practical to use the Improved Clinch Knot.  It is difficult to tighten this knot with heavy mono, so another knot, such as the Buffer Loop Knot, should be employed.  Moistening the Improved Clinch Knot with saliva helps to tighten it.

**Fig. 1** Pass the line end through the hook eye.  Put about six inches of line through the eye so there will be ample line to tie the knot.

**Fig. 2** Hold the fly securely in one hand and wrap the line end five times around the standing part of the line, as shown in the illustration. Now pass the line end back through the small loop near the hook eye, and also through the large loop.

**Fig. 3** The finished Improved Clinch Knot, tightened and trimmed.

## SHOCKER KNOT

Often a fly fisherman needs a heavy length of nylon monofilament at one end of his leader to act as a "shock tippet." For fish such as sailfish, snook and northern pike, "shock tippets" of 60-pound mono or heavier are absolutely necessary if the angler wants to hold the fish he hooks.

The Shocker Knot is a very fast way to join a light leader (normally 12- to 20-pound test) to a piece of heavy nylon. Many experienced fly-rodders consider the "Shocker Knot" a simple, fast knot to tie with superior knot strength.

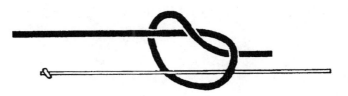

**Fig. 1** Make an Overhand Knot in the light leader end. Form a loose Overhand Knot in the heavy line and pass the end of the light line through the Overhand Knot.

**Fig. 2** Tighten the Overhand Knot in the heavy line.

**172**

**Fig. 3** Make three to five wraps with the light line around the heavy line, and pass the end back through the first loop. Pull on the light line ends until the wraps jam against the Overhand Knot in the heavy line. Then firmly pull on all line ends and trim close.

*Bob McNally battles a sailfish on fly tackle. Fly gear is well up to handling huge marine fish, provided the angler has tied his leader-line-backing knots with care.*

**173**

## KNOTTING BACKING TO FLY LINE

Although this knot takes a little time to tie, it's extremely secure and will pass through rod guides easily, which is important when fighting bonefish, sailfish and other fast, far-running species.

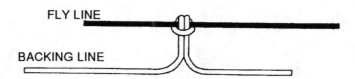

**Fig. 1** Tie a simple Square Knot with the fly line and backing line.

**Fig. 2** Pull the fly line straight, and tug the backing line downward.

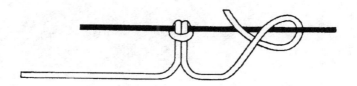

**Fig. 3** Pull the Square Knot tight, and tie six Half-Hitches onto the fly line with the short end of the backing.

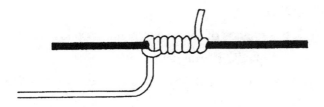

**Fig. 4** Pull the Half-Hitches tight, and trim the short end of the backing line.

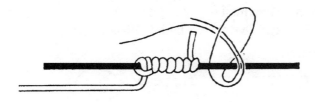

**Fig. 5** Wrap the knot with 00 nylon thread, and continue over the knot, wrapping the short end of the fly line to the backing line.

**Fig. 6** After wrapping, or "whip-finishing" the connection with thread, coat the entire knot with Pliobond rubber cement or lacquer.

**175**

## SPLICED LOOP

While this method of forming a fly line loop is bulkier than some other methods, it's still popular with some anglers because the Spliced Loop is extremely strong when properly tied.

**Fig. 1** Remove one inch of the fly line coating from the end of the line, and also one inch of coating three inches from the end of the line. This can be done with nail polish remover.

**Fig. 2** Form the loop and with size 00 nylon thread tightly wrap over the two pieces of fly line that have had the coating removed. Varnish or lacquer the completed splice, or coat it with Pliobond.

## ROLLING SPLICE

This isn't the easiest splice to learn for joining backing line to a fly line. However, it is one of the most secure.

The Rolling Splice can be made by one person, but it's much easier if an assistant holds the free end of the fly line, while the first person actually makes the splice.

**176**

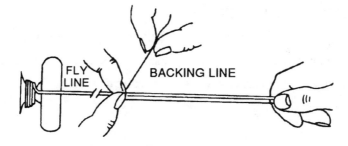

**Fig. 1** Tie the fly line loosely to a door knob (or other secure object), leaving about two feet of line to work with. Lay the backing next to the fly line, and begin wrapping three inches from the end of the fly line. Wind the backing tightly onto the fly line, and wrap to within 1/4-inch of the fly line end.

**Fig. 2** Now lay in a piece of fine nylon thread, and continue wrapping over the fly line and onto the backing line. Complete the splice with a whip finish by putting the end of the backing line in the nylon thread loop, and pulling the two free ends of the thread. This will draw the backing line out in a reverse direction and secure the wrapping.

**Fig. 3** This is how the finished splice looks after the loose ends have been trimmed. Pliobond cement or lacquer should be applied.

**177**

## QUICK FLY LINE SPLICE

This splice is particularly popular among anglers who design their own shooting-head fly lines. This splice is easier to tie than it looks, and makes for a good, permanent connection.

1 ¹/₄

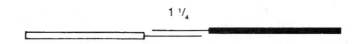

**Fig. 1** Remove the coating of 1 1/4-inch of fly line with acetone or nail polish remover, then place lines next to each other.

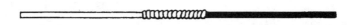

**Fig. 2** With nylon thread, wind the two lines together, as shown. Make sure the nylon wraps are tight. Complete the splice by coating with varnish or Pliobond.

## BLOOD KNOT

The Blood Knot is the most widely used knot among fly fishermen for joining lengths of nylon monofilament when making tapered leaders.

The Blood Knot is easy to tie. It's extremely strong when made properly. Moreover, it is especially valuable to fly rodders because it is a small knot and runs through rod guides with ease.

Only lines of nearly equal diameters should be joined with the Blood Knot, which insures peak strength from the knot.

**178**

**Fig. 1** Cross the two lines, and wrap one line three times around the other. Now place the line end through the loop formed by the two lines.

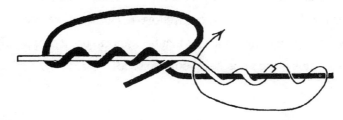

**Fig. 2** Turn the other line around the first line three times, put its end through the loop from the opposite side.

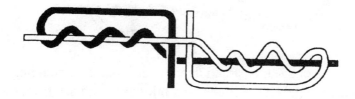

**Fig. 3** The turns should look like this. Now slowly pull on both long ends of the lines.

**Fig. 4** The tightened knot looks like this, loose ends trimmed.

## EXTENSION BLOOD KNOT

This is the strongest and most popular way to attach "dropper lines" for fishing two or more flies simultaneously.

Often the Extension Blood Knot is not as convenient to tie as some other dropper knots. For example, if the fly fishing leader is already "made up," it must be cut and rejoined if an Extension Blood Knot is to be employed. But when an angler knows while making his leader that he wants to use a dropper fly or two—this is the knot that should be used.

**Fig. 1** Wind one leader strand three times around the standing part of the second leader strand, and bring the end back behind the first turn. Do the same with the other leader end, and the knot should appear as in the drawing.

180

**Fig. 2** Pull on the standing part of both leader strands to draw the knot tight. Trim only one of the tag ends of the knot. The other tag end becomes the dropper line for attaching a fly. Usually it's best to keep dropper lines short, less than 1-foot in length, to prevent tangling while fishing.

## HUFFNAGLE KNOT

This is a knot recently developed in South Florida and is an excellent one for tying a light line to a heavy one. There are a number of knots similar to the Huffnagle, but this one is currently at the top of the evolutionary ladder and is a good one for fly anglers to put into their repertoire of knot tying skills. It's shown here being made with a Bimini Twist from a "class" fly tippet to a heavier shock tippet, a good use for this simple, very strong connection.

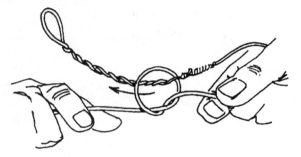

**Fig. 1** Tie an Overhand knot with the heavy line and place the light line (in this case a Bimini Twist) through it.

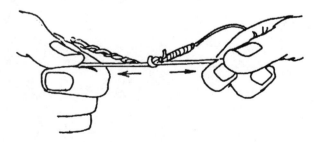

**Fig. 2** Tighten the Overhand Knot so it "jams" against the Bimini Twist wraps.

**182**

**Fig. 3** Tie an Overhand Knot with the light line and tighten so it "jams" against the Overhand Knot in the heavy line.

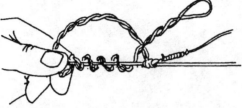

**Fig. 4** Make a large loop with the lighter line, then wrap the lighter line around the heavy line as shown in the  illustration.

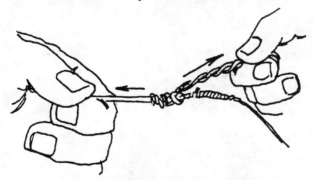

**Fig. 5** Pull all tag and standing ends tight, moistening line wraps so they seat together smoothly and securely.

**Fig. 6** The finished Huffnagle Knot with tag ends trimmed close.

**183**

*Wire leaders are needed for big, fast barracuda, which have razor-edged teeth. This one was caught by charter captain John Campbell.*

# 6 Wire, Cable Connections

Heavy nylon monofilament line is the best leader material for most fishing. However, for some angling wire must be used. Wire line is often needed in deep trolling, and wire leaders are used frequently by anglers after pike and muskies. Moreover, wire leaders are a virtual necessity for much marine angling when bluefish, mackerel, barracuda and other "toothy critters" are the targets.

Generally, there are three types of wire—nylon-coated wire cable, single-strand wire and uncoated wire cable. Tying knots with any of these wires, or connecting fishing lines to them, presents some very special and difficult problems.

Most of the knots and connections that can be used with ordinary fishing lines and leaders cannot be used with wire. Such metal is too stiff, and has too much tendency to kink. Fortunately, many special wire "wraps" have been developed over the years that hold well, even under the extreme pressures exerted by large, ocean-roaming gamefish.

## HAYWIRE TWIST

This is one of the best and most commonly-used methods for linking solid wire to any type of connecting ring. The number of wraps and the two different **kinds** of wraps in the Haywire Twist may seem elaborate to many anglers. But for numerous varieties of strong saltwater fish, this tie is absolutely necessary to keep the wire from "pulling out."

**Fig. 1** Thread the end of the wire through the hook eye, pulling about five inches of wire through it.

**Fig. 2** Pinch the two pieces of wire together, and begin twisting the wire strands **simultaneously** together, so they wrap around each other at about a 45-degree angle. Make four to six "wraps."

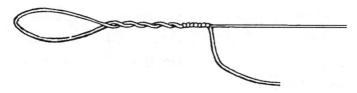

**Fig. 3** Now bend the tag end of the wire at a 90-degree angle to the standing part of wire, and begin making "barrel wraps" tight to each other, as shown in the illustration. Make four to six "barrel wraps." Bend the tag end of the wire back and forth until it breaks, and the Haywire Twist is completed.

**187**

## RIG FOR CUT BAIT

This is an elaborate method of fastening a hook with a wire leader for use in trolling cut bait for large gamefish. It's an excellent, strong rig that also can be used for trolling whole dead baits like mullet, ballyhoo or even in freshwater with suckers or shiners for muskies or bass.

The wire is inserted through the hook eye and wrapped around the hook shank six or seven times. Then its end is brought back out the hook eye, and a standard Haywire Twist is made. The tag end of the wire is left protruding from the Haywire Twist like a "pin." This "pin" is used to keep the bait secured to the hook.

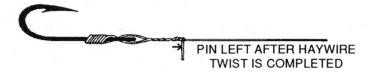

PIN LEFT AFTER HAYWIRE
TWIST IS COMPLETED

## SINGLE-SLEEVE RIG

To rig this connection thread wire through a metal sleeve, pass the wire through the hook eye, then back through the sleeve. Crimp the sleeve and trim the tag end of the wire.

The Single-Sleeve Rig is one of the most popular ways of connecting wire to a hook eye or lure. It's commonly used by saltwater anglers for light inshore fishing.

Wire and metal sleeves are available at most well-stocked tackle shops.

## JOINING WIRE TO FISHING LINE

This connection is used by anglers who want to tie wire leaders to braided or monofilament fishing line.

It can be difficult to make if care is not taken because the wire can kink, which ruins the tie.

**Fig. 1** Tie a loop in the end of the fishing line. Put the wire end through the loop and wrap the end around one side of the loop.

**Fig. 2** Wind the wire completely around the loop twice.

**Fig. 3** Bring the wire back out through the loop, and wrap it four times around the standing part of the wire.

**189**

## OVERHAND WIRE WRAP
### (Also called Barrel Twist)

This is merely the second part of the Haywire Twist. The wire end is put through the hook eye and wrapped around the standing part of the wire four or five times at a 90-degree angle.

The Overhand Wire Wrap is a satisfactory connection for light fishing, such as trolling for pike, Spanish mackerel or bluefish. However, when large fish are the target, the Haywire Twist or Single Sleeve Rig is preferred.

## METAL SLEEVE SECURING WIRE LOOP

This is a variation of the Single-Sleeve Rig. It can be used to connect wire to a hook or lure "eye," or it can be used to form a simple wire loop to which a leader or line may be attached.

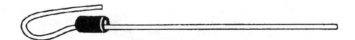

**Fig. 1** Pass the wire through the sleeve and double the wire back toward the sleeve.

**Fig. 2** Put the wire through the sleeve again, leaving the size loop desired.

**Fig. 3** Turn the end of the wire back into the sleeve.

**Fig. 4** Crimp the sleeve firmly and the connection is finished.

## QUICK-CHANGE WIRE WRAP

The Quick-Change Wire Wrap is the ideal connection for anglers who need a wire wrap for use with light tackle, yet want the convenience of being able to change lures quickly.

Although this wire wrap is not as strong as some other wire connections, such as the Haywire Twist, it's adequate for most freshwater fishing, and even light saltwater angling.

The trick to making the Quick-Change Wire Wrap is to make the "wraps" of the wire end onto the standing part of the wire somewhat apart. The wide wraps make the tie much stronger than if "tight" wraps were used. Also, because the wraps are made far apart, the connection is easy to unravel. Thus a lure can be put on or taken off very quickly.

## SAFETY-PIN RIG

The Safety-Pin Rig is an excellent way of attaching wire to a large hook for use in trolling "strip baits."

The wire should be threaded through the hook eye. Four large wraps are made around the standing part of the wire, followed by five or six "tight" wraps, much like making a standard Haywire Twist.

The final step is the most important. Bend the wire end straight up from the standing part of the wire, bending it again at a right angle to the standing part, and then bend a small U-shape into the wire's end.

Bending the wire is done most easily with needle-nose pliers.

SAFETY PIN MADE
WITH WIRE LEADER

**193**

## METAL SLEEVE AND KNOT

This is a great connection for joining heavy wire, cable or even heavy-test monofilament to a hook. It's adequate for most types of saltwater trolling, but this is a permanent tie that is most practical when used with trolling outfits that will not be "broken down" after each day's use.

**Fig. 1** Thread the wire through the sleeve and hook eye.

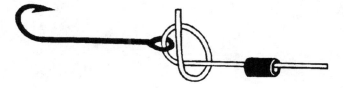

**Fig. 2** Wrap the end of the wire around the standing part of the wire.

**Fig. 3** Pass the end through the hook eye again.

**194**

**Fig. 4** Now bring the wire end through the open loop, through the sleeve, crimp the sleeve tight, and trim the excess wire.

---

## DOUBLE-SLEEVE RIG

This connection is slightly more elaborate than a Single-Sleeve Rig. But the Double-Sleeve Rig is much stronger, so it's favored by many anglers for attaching cable to large hooks for big-game offshore trolling.

To make the connection, insert the wire through two sleeves. Pass the end through the hook eye, then back through one sleeve. Now wrap the wire end once around the standing part of the wire, and push the end through the second sleeve. Crimp both sleeves and trim the excess wire end.

**195**

## KNOTTING NYLON-COATED WIRE TO MONOFILAMENT

Many veteran anglers believe this is the most secure knot for connecting nylon-coated wire line to monofilament. It also can be used for joining single-strand wire to monofilament, so long as care is made not to kink the wire.

This connection is very similar to the Albright Special. It's important when making this tie to keep the wire straight while the knot is pulled tight. This keeps the wire from kinking when monofilament wraps are drawn tight.

**Fig. 1** Form a loop with the wire line and a loop with the mono line. Place the two loops on top of each other, as shown.

**Fig. 2** Wrap the monofilament line six times around the wire loop. Then insert the mono end through the wire loop.

**Fig. 3** To tighten the knot, slowly pull on the standing parts of both the mono and wire lines.

**Fig. 4** The finished, trimmed connection.

*Some toothy freshwater fish like muskies require the use of wire leaders.*

## SPECIAL SPOON WRAP
### (Sometimes called Trolling Spoon Wrap)

This is an excellent way of attaching wire to a spoon or other artificial lure. The Special Spoon Wrap forms a wire loop through the lure's connecting ring and allows the lure to "swim" in a lifelike fashion.

This wire connection is used by many guides for such fish as pike, lake trout, muskies, king mackerel and wahoo.

**Fig. 1** Put the wire end through the lure's connecting hole or ring twice, leaving about five inches of wire to make the connection.

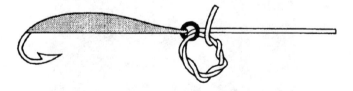

**Fig. 2** Wrap the wire end four times around the wire circle formed through the lure's connecting ring.

**198**

**Fig. 3** Wind the wire end loosely around the standing part of the wire twice, then make several tight wraps around the standing wire, similar to the way a Haywire Twist is made.

## FIGURE EIGHT KNOT

Although the Figure Eight Knot is recommended only in emergency situations when used with nylon monofilament or braided line, it's a very secure tie when used with braided wire.

The Figure Eight Knot is employed often by anglers using braided wire line when deep jigging for toothy fish, like snapper.

**Fig. 1** Put the wire end through the hook or lure "eye." Bring the end back and wind it once around the standing part of the wire, then insert the end through the loop formed in front of the hook eye.

**Fig. 2** The Figure Eight Knot after it has been drawn tight.

**199**

### BALLYHOO RIG

This is a standard method for rigging a hook with wire when trolling offshore with ballyhoo bait.

It's easy to prepare this rig, and it's very practical. First, affix a small, 8-inch piece of soft "rigging wire" to the hook eye with an Overhand Wire Wrap. Next, attach a wire leader to the hook eye with a Haywire Twist.

It's important to leave a small 1/2-inch tag end of wire after the Haywire Twist is completed. The wire tag end is used to hold the ballyhoo onto the hook by its beak or nose.

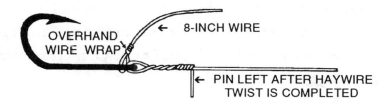

OVERHAND WIRE WRAP · ← 8-INCH WIRE · ← PIN LEFT AFTER HAYWIRE TWIST IS COMPLETED

### CIRCLE WRAP WITH DOUBLE SLEEVE
**(Also called Big Game Cable Loop)**

This is **the** connection to use when securing multi-strand wire or cable to a hook for big game trolling. This wrap, when properly made, withstands tremendous stress that even huge sharks can create.

To make the connection, insert the cable or wire through two metal sleeves and then through the hook eye twice, forming a small, 1/2-inch diameter loop. Wrap the wire end around the loop four times, then insert the end of the wire

**200**

through the first sleeve, and crimp the sleeve. Wind the wire
end twice around the standing part of the wire, insert the end
through the second sleeve, and crimp it.

## MATCH METHOD
### (Also called Heated Twist)

This is a very quick way to secure a lure or hook to
nylon-coated wire, and when properly done it's a very durable,
strong connection.

The Match Method is easy. Merely push the end of
the nylon-coated wire through the hook, lure or swivel "eye."
Then make five twists around the standing part of the wire
with the wire end. Now light a match and pass it back and
forth quickly under the wire wraps. When the nylon coating
begins to melt and fuse, remove the match. After the nylon
cools, the connection is complete.

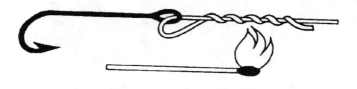

*An everyday fishing situation, like using bait for catfish, may demand special knots to prepare certain rigs.*

# Knots In Everyday Fishing Rigs

Knowing how to tie knots is a skill needed by every fisherman.  However, if the fisherman does not know how to apply his knot-tying knowledge, if he does not understand when and where to employ specific knots in rigging different tackle, then his knot-tying expertise is of little value.

This chapter presents concrete examples of how to use acceptable knots in everyday fishing situations.

The knots shown in the following fishing rigs were selected because they are commonly used by expert anglers. However, there is duplication of purpose in many knots, and while a Bimini Twist may be shown as performing one function, a Spider Hitch, for example, could be substituted.

Usually more than one kind of knot is needed when putting together any fishing rig. This chapter illustrates the different knots that can be used with various fishing rigs. The rigs presented here also are of tremendous value to fishermen faced with specific angling presentation needs.

*Using the right rig is vital to walleye fishing success.*

## HEAVY-DUTY FLY LEADER

Some of the same knots are used in making this leader as are used in making a Light, Freshwater Leader. But different lengths and tests of nylon monofilament are necessary in making a Heavy-Duty Fly Leader. This leader is excellent for fish such as snook, barracuda, northern pike and muskellunge. Note, however, that the "shock tippet" may range from 30- to 100-pound test—depending on the angling situation at hand and the species sought.

A Fast Nail Knot (or other type Nail Knot) should be used to secure the permanent butt section of the leader to the fly line. Then all the other leader sections are joined with Blood Knots. The "shock tippet" is connected to the 12-pound test nylon with a Shocker Knot. The Shocker Knot is used because it is an excellent knot for tying two pieces of mono together that are of different diameters. The Homer Rhode Loop is used at the fly because it can be tied readily with heavy nylon. Too, the "loop" it forms through the fly's hook eye permits the best possible action of the fly when retrieved.

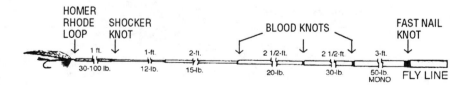

HOMER
RHODE   SHOCKER                                    FAST NAIL
LOOP    KNOT            BLOOD KNOTS                KNOT
  1 ft.        1-ft.   2-ft.   2 1/2-ft.   2 1/2-ft.   3-ft.
  30-100 lb.   12-lb.  15-lb.    20-lb.      30-lb.   50-lb.
                                                      MONO   FLY LINE

### RIGGING A BAITFISH FOR DEEP TROLLING

Many skilled anglers are familiar with this rig, especially saltwater fishermen because it's an excellent way to present baits to billfish, mackerel, and other offshore species. The rig also can be used for heavyweight muskies, lake trout and pike.

When a large baitfish is used, like a mullet, a deboning tool is employed and the bait's entrails also are removed. This gives the bait additional action when trolled.

The hook is positioned in the bait's belly cut so the hook eye is just inside its mouth. A 2- to 4-ounce egg sinker is threaded with wire leader, and the wire end is then pushed up through the fish's lower jaw, through the hook eye and finally out the top of the bait's head. A Haywire Twist is put in the wire.

The final step is to take a heavy duty-needle and stout thread and sew the bait's mouth and slit belly closed.

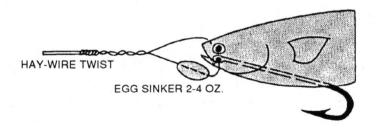

HAY-WIRE TWIST

EGG SINKER 2-4 OZ.

**206**

## DEEP TROLLING SPOON AND WIRE LEADER

This rig is used by Great Lakes and saltwater anglers who want to get a trolled spoon or other lure deep while fishing for lake trout, salmon, walleyes, mackerel and wahoo. The wire leader helps keep the rig down, and fish with sharp teeth can't cut it.

To make this outfit, attach a pinch-on sinker about one foot from the fishing line end, and slip a trolling keel onto the line (the trolling keel helps prevent line twist, as well as takes the lure deep).

Attach a barrel swivel to the end of the fishing line with an Offshore Swivel Knot. Next connect the wire leader to the swivel with an Overhand Wire Wrap, which is adequate for most light trolling situations. Use the Special Spoon Wrap to fasten the spoon to the wire. The Special Spoon Wrap will allow the spoon to wobble freely and lifelike while trolled.

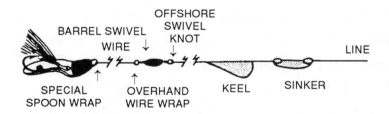

**207**

## BOTTOM RIG

This bottom bait fishing rig is common among surf anglers, as well as bank fishermen in fresh and saltwater. A sinker of appropriate weight should be used to effectively hold the rig on bottom. In saltwater surf, or in strong river current, a pyramid sinker is most effective. This rig is employed often by anglers after catfish and surf fish such as red drum and bluefish.

Usually heavy line is needed for casting and fishing in the surf or strong river current, because large sinkers are needed to hold bait on bottom. For this reason, the Jansik Special is the perfect knot for securing the fishing line to the 3-way swivel. The Jansik Special is a very strong knot and is easy to tie with heavy monofilament.

A loop should be formed in the leader that runs to the sinker and connected to the 3-way swivel with a Lark's Head Knot. The Lark's Head Knot can be tied quickly and it holds well. The other end of the leader is connected to the sinker "eye" with a Jansik Special. The leader connecting the swivel to the sinker should be made with line 20 percent less in strength than the fishing line and the leader attached to the hook. This is so if the sinker becomes fouled on bottom, usually only the sinker leader will be broken when the angler pulls hard—so the entire fishing rig is not lost, which makes re-rigging easier.

**208**

Finally, a hook is snelled to a leader of the same test as the fishing line, a loop is formed at the other end of the leader, and the loop is connected to the 3-way swivel with a Lark's Head Knot.

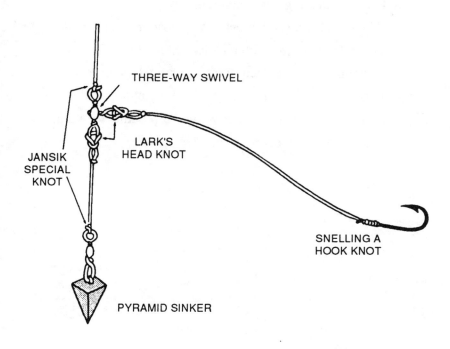

THREE-WAY SWIVEL

LARK'S HEAD KNOT

JANSIK SPECIAL KNOT

SNELLING A HOOK KNOT

PYRAMID SINKER

**209**

## RIGGING A MONO "SHOCK LEADER"

This is one of the most popular rigs for tying a "shock leader" to fishing line.

When a "shock leader" is needed for certain types of fishing, the first thing that should be done is to form a doubled line at the end of the fishing line (a doubled line assures 100 percent efficiency from knots, and doubles the line end where the most wear from fishing occurs). The Spider Hitch is a superb knot for creating a doubled line.

The heavy, monofilament "shock leader" then should be tied to the doubled line with an Albright Special. Finally, the lure is connected to the heavy mono with a Homer Rhode Loop. This knot can be tied easily with heavy nylon, and it allows a lure to "swim" more lifelike than if the line were tied tightly to the lure's connecting ring.

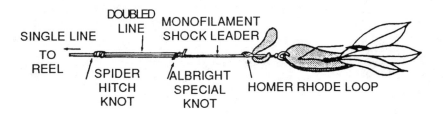

**210**

## TWO LURES ON A 3-WAY SWIVEL

This is a good rig for fishing two lures simultaneously. Usually a surface lure or a floating-diving plug is used in conjunction with a deep-running lure—such as a lead-head jig. When the rig is retrieved, the two lures travel at different depths, and their leaders are unlikely to tangle.

This 3-way swivel rig also is used by anglers fishing for school fish, such as crappies, white bass and spotted seatrout. Many times when one fish is hooked another will strike the second lure as it's pulled through the water by the first fish.

Both lures can be tied to their leaders with a Dave Hawk's Drop-Loop Knot. This is a good, strong, easy-to-tie knot that will permit both lures to vibrate and wiggle freely.

All three lines tied to the 3-way swivel can be knotted with an Eye-Crosser Knot. The Eye-Crosser Knot has excellent knot strength and is quickly made.

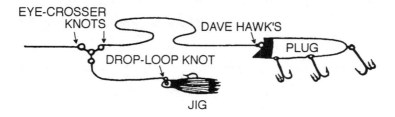

EYE-CROSSER KNOTS
DAVE HAWK'S
PLUG
DROP-LOOP KNOT
JIG

**211**

## RIGGING A BALLYHOO FOR TROLLING

The ballyhoo is a small beakfish considered one of the best natural baits for mackerel, billfish, dolphin and other offshore sportfish.

Rigging A Ballyhoo For Trolling is quite different from preparing any other type bait. But once learned it's a fast, simple method of using natural bait offshore. First, the hook should be prepared with the special Ballyhoo Rig, as shown, using a size 5/0 to 10/0 hook (depending on bait size). Next, the hook point should be worked under one side of the bait's gills and maneuvered far back into the body cavity. Work the hook point out under the bait, and pull on it until the hook eye is positioned under the bait's gill cover. Now push the wire "pin" up through the center of the bait's jaws and out the top of the head in front of the eyes.

While holding the hook eye firmly to the bait's "chin," wind the light, 8-inch copper wire tightly around the bait's head, down the ballyhoo's beak, and over the leader wire. Be sure to wrap the copper wire several times around the "pin" on the bait's head, which helps hold the wire in position. Make the copper wire wraps tight and snug, finishing near the bait's bill.

If the bait spins when trolled, usually a small knife slit made in the ballyhoo's belly just forward of the hook point will remove tension there, and will make the bait track straight without spinning.

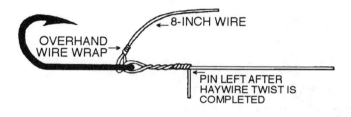

OVERHAND WIRE WRAP

8-INCH WIRE

PIN LEFT AFTER HAYWIRE TWIST IS COMPLETED

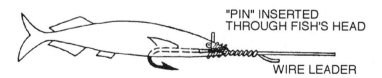

"PIN" INSERTED THROUGH FISH'S HEAD

WIRE LEADER

**213**

## RIGGING A MONO LEADER TO BRAIDED LINE

This is the way some bait-casters attach a monofilament leader to braided casting line. The rig is good for light or medium-heavy fresh or saltwater angling.

A loop is formed at one end of the mono leader with a Perfection Loop Knot. Then the braided line is joined to the loop with a Multiple Clinch Knot. An Improved Clinch Knot should be used to attach the mono leader to a snap swivel, and the lure then is snapped to the swivel.

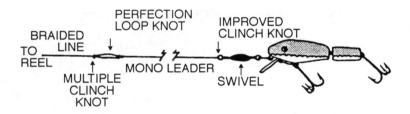

PERFECTION
LOOP KNOT

IMPROVED
CLINCH KNOT

BRAIDED
TO LINE
REEL

MONO LEADER

MULTIPLE
CLINCH
KNOT

SWIVEL

**214**

## NEW ZEALAND OFFSHORE TROLLING RIG

Few big game, offshore saltwater anglers use this trolling rig. Yet it's a good one and can be made very quickly.

The hook should already be rigged to the leader and rod-reel, then the live bait is "sewn" onto the hook.

The hook is "sewn" to the jaws or through the nostrils of a natural bait, such as a bonito. After each wrap around the hook's bend a Half-Hitch should be made with the twine.

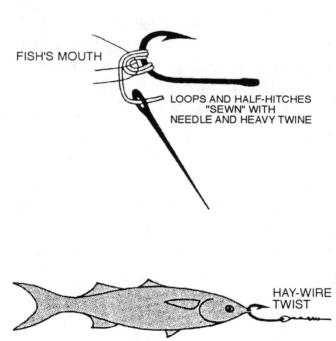

FISH'S MOUTH

LOOPS AND HALF-HITCHES
"SEWN" WITH
NEEDLE AND HEAVY TWINE

HAY-WIRE
TWIST

## SPREADER RIG FOR NATURAL BAITS

This natural bait rig can be used for many kinds of fresh and saltwater fish.

The first thing to do when making this rig is to purchase a wire "spreader" of a size most suitable to the type fishing desired.

Because bottom bait rigs often become fouled on bottom, the Improved Berkley Trilene Knot should be used when tying the fishing line to the center swivel "eye" of the "spreader," and also when connecting the two nylon monofilament leaders to the "spreader." The Improved Berkley Trilene Knot will hold up very well under the stresses caused by pulling heavily on the line to free bottom-fouled hooks.

Both bait hooks should be joined to the two leaders with the Snelling A Hook Knot. Snelled hook knots are very strong and they give a good direct pull from line to hook, which is essential for consistently hooking bottomfish.

The sinker in this rigging is joined to a light leader with the Figure Eight Knot. The sinker leader then is tied to the "spreader" with a Figure Eight Knot, because this weak knot **will break** should the sinker foul on bottom. If a break occurs, only the sinker is lost—not the entire rig.

**216**

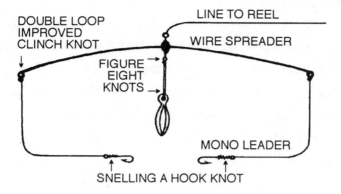

DOUBLE LOOP
IMPROVED
CLINCH KNOT

LINE TO REEL

WIRE SPREADER

FIGURE
EIGHT
KNOTS

MONO LEADER

SNELLING A HOOK KNOT

## STRIP-BAIT TROLLING RIG

Although there are many ways to rig strip or "cut" baits for trolling, many savvy saltwater anglers consider this one the best. The rig is strong, allows the bait to have plenty of "action" in the water, and it can be made quickly.

To prepare this rig, first connect the fishing line to a heavy-duty swivel, using an Improved Clinch Knot. Then, join one end of a 7-foot wire leader to the swivel with a Haywire Twist. Finally, fasten the wire leader end to the hook with a Safety-Pin Rig, then attach the strip bait.

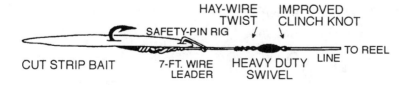

HAY-WIRE
TWIST
SAFETY-PIN RIG

IMPROVED
CLINCH KNOT

TO REEL

CUT STRIP BAIT

7-FT. WIRE
LEADER

HEAVY DUTY
SWIVEL

LINE

**217**

## POPPING CORK RIG

The Popping Cork Rig is excellent when angling for fish such as seatrout, snook and red drum (redfish). At times this rig also is excellent for bass, stripers and even crappies. The cork is a specially-designed float. It is "popped" by the angler when he raises his rod tip sharply during the retrieve. Such surface commotion attracts gamefish to the jig or other lure attached below the popping cork. The cork also can signal strikes to the angler. Natural baits such as minnows and live shrimp also can be used effectively with this rig.

While the Popping Cork is best in shallow water, under 6-feet deep, at times open-water species like striped bass can be taken in deep water when linesides are herding bait near the surface.

To make this rig, attach a commercially-made Popping Cork about 1-foot from the end of the fishing line. Join the end of the line to a barrel swivel with the strong, simple-to-tie, Improved Clinch Knot.

Next, use the Crawford Knot to join a heavy, 2-foot "shock tippet" to the other end of the barrel swivel. A "shock tippet" is needed when after fish with sharp teeth or gill covers, and the Crawford Knot is excellent for tying heavy monofilament securely.

Finally, use the McNally Loop to tie a jig or other lure to the "shock tippet." This loop is not difficult to make with heavy line, yet has good knot strength.

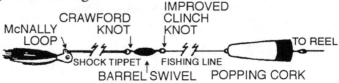

**218**

## 3-WAY SWIVEL DEEP RIG

This rig can be made in just a few minutes. It's used most often by freshwater anglers trolling deep for fish such as walleyes, bass and pike. It's also an excellent rig for deep fishing in current.

Deep lures frequently "hang-up" on bottom. The advantage to this rig is that the dipsey sinker usually fouls and not the lure—especially if it's a floating-diving plug. Because the sinker is tied to the 3-way swivel with a weak Figure Eight Knot and a length of line lighter than the fishing line, the line to the sinker will break—not the line connecting the lure.

In making this rig, the fishing line is fastened to a 3-way swivel with a Berkley Trilene Knot. A short piece of monofilament line is tied to another ring of the 3-way swivel, and to a barrel swivel, using Berkley Trilene Knots. Berkley Trilene Knots are used because they have excellent knot strength, which is needed for this trolling rig.

A Nail Loop is used to tie the lure to the monofilament leader. The Nail Loop is a superb "loop knot" that's easy to tie with monofilament testing up to about 50-pounds, and allows a lure to have the best possible action when trolled. The dipsey sinker is fastened to the 3-way swivel with a short piece of light monofilament, and Figure Eight Knots are used.

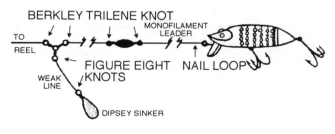

219

## DEEP TROLLING RIG

This rig is used primarily for trolling natural marine baits, such as mullet or ballyhoo over reefs for bottomfish such as amberjacks and grouper. However, spoons and jigs can be used instead of natural baits, and the rig is useful for some freshwater trolling for lake trout, salmon, walleyes and pike.

To make this rig, tie a permanent doubled line at the end of the fishing line, using the durable Bimini Twist. The doubled line from the Bimini will guarantee 100-percent knot strength in the line-to-wire connection.

Tie a 3-foot length of wire to the doubled line with the Joining Wire to Fishing Line Knot, and fasten the other end of the wire to a heavy, 6-ounce trolling sinker with a Haywire Twist.

Next, join a 6-foot piece of wire to the other end of the trolling sinker, using a Haywire Twist, and attach the opposite end of the wire to a large hook (or lure) using a Double-Sleeve Rig. Both the Haywire Twist and the Double-Sleeve Rig are superb connections for wire.

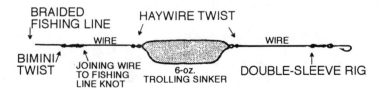

## LIGHT, FRESHWATER FLY LEADER

Few anglers know how to make a fly leader properly. The fly leader is extremely important both for casting and presenting a fly to fish. In the illustration, the length and pound test of each leader section is shown for the best construction of a freshwater leader.

A Fast Nail Knot is used to tie the permanent leader butt to the fly line because it is the quickest, easiest Nail Knot to tie and, too, it goes through rod guides readily. The lengths of leader material are joined with Blood Knots. The Blood Knot is simple to tie, it's strong, and makes a small connection. The Extension Blood Knot, although it takes more time to tie than some other knots, is the most dependable for attaching "dropper leaders" so that more than one fly can be fished simultaneously. The Improved Clinch Knot is an excellent choice for tying a light nylon monofilament leader to a fly.

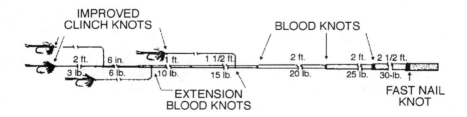

IMPROVED
CLINCH KNOTS

BLOOD KNOTS

2 ft.  6 in.  1 ft.  1 1/2 ft.  2 ft.  2 ft.  2 1/2 ft.
3 lb.  6 lb.  10 lb.  15 lb.  20 lb.  25 lb.  30-lb.

EXTENSION
BLOOD KNOTS

FAST NAIL
KNOT

**221**

## OFFSHORE WIRE LEADER

To make this rig, first form a double line with the fishing line by making the strong, easily-tied Spider Hitch. Then connect the doubled line to a heavy-duty barrel swivel, using a Palomar Knot. This knot is recommended because it's easy to tie with a doubled line, yet is very strong. Join the desired length of wire to the hook and to the swivel with Haywire Twists.

Wire leaders of this type are used frequently by saltwater anglers fishing for mackerel, bluefish and other species with sharp teeth. This leader set-up also is a good one for anglers after heavy pike and muskies.

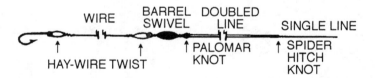

222

*Giant tarpon demand that terminal-tackle rigs be of superior quality and strength.*

**223**

## COAT HANGER BAIT RIG FOR REEF FISHING

This is an old and reliable bait rig when bottom fishing for grouper, snapper, amberjack, and even giant catfish. Different versions of this rig can be adapted according to the kind and size fish sought, ocean or river current speed, and bottom conditions. The value of the Coat Hanger Bait Rig is that a live bait can be fished at any depth without it tangling with the sinker or fishing line.

The rig isn't as difficult to make as the illustration might indicate. First take the fishing line and make a doubled line, using the Surgeon's Loop. Then tie the doubled line to a heavy-duty snap swivel with a Double Improved Clinch Knot, and coat both knots with rubber cement or Pliobond.

Next step is to rig the coat hanger. Pinch the two ends of a coat hanger closed with pliers, and wrap them tightly with wire. Then, with pliers, bend the hanger "neck" into a tight loop.

Attach a 10- or 12-foot wire leader to one end of the coat hanger, using a Haywire Twist. Run the wire through the loop made in the coat hanger "neck," and fasten the bait hook to the end of the wire with another Haywire Twist.

Take a length of line that's lighter than the fishing line, and tie it to the other end of the coat hanger with a Figure Eight Knot, as shown. Make a Single Overhand Loop in the opposite end of the light-test line, and fasten the loop to a heavy sinker using the Lark's Head Knot.

**224**

Hook the live bait through the lips, attach the snap swivel on the fishing line to the end of the coat hanger—and the rig is ready for fishing.

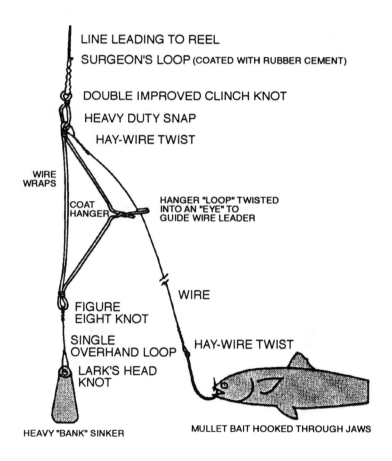

LINE LEADING TO REEL

SURGEON'S LOOP (COATED WITH RUBBER CEMENT)

DOUBLE IMPROVED CLINCH KNOT

HEAVY DUTY SNAP

HAY-WIRE TWIST

WIRE WRAPS

COAT HANGER

HANGER "LOOP" TWISTED INTO AN "EYE" TO GUIDE WIRE LEADER

WIRE

FIGURE EIGHT KNOT

SINGLE OVERHAND LOOP

HAY-WIRE TWIST

LARK'S HEAD KNOT

HEAVY "BANK" SINKER

MULLET BAIT HOOKED THROUGH JAWS

**225**

## PLUG WITH A SMALL TRAILING SPOON

When fishing is tough, it's often productive to try this rig, fishing two different types of lures simultaneously. A large surface plug is tied to the fishing line, and a small spoon or jig is attached to a piece of monofilament that's tied to the connecting ring of the larger plug's rear hook.

By fishing this rig, you may be able to determine what size or type lure the fish want, at what depth the fish are feeding, and what color lure they prefer.

The Duncan Loop should be used to tie the large plug and smaller lure to the two monofilament fishing lines. Each lure will "swim" freely on the loop during the retrieve.

The Clinch Knot is an adequate tie for connecting the trailing leader to the rear hook ring on the plug.

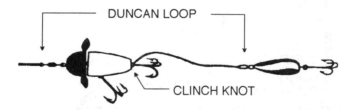

DUNCAN LOOP

CLINCH KNOT

**226**

## FEATHER-STRIP TROLLING RIG

The Feather-Strip Trolling Rig is deadly for many species of saltwater gamefish. The rig combines the fish-attracting qualities of a feather head and the "smell" of a natural bait cut into strips.

The rig is simple to put together. Make a Haywire Twist at one end of a 6-foot wire leader, and connect the Haywire Twist to the monofilament fishing line with an Albright Special Knot. Next, pass the wire leader end through the hole in the feather head. Join the hook to the wire leader with the Rig For Cut Bait, and attach the strip bait as shown in the illustration.

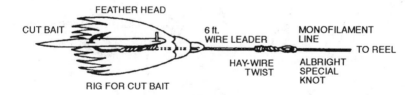

**227**

## BASIC FRESHWATER BAIT RIGS

## RIGS

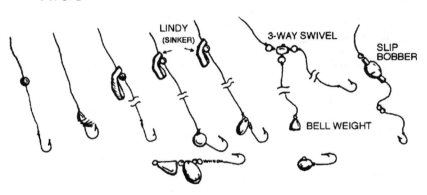

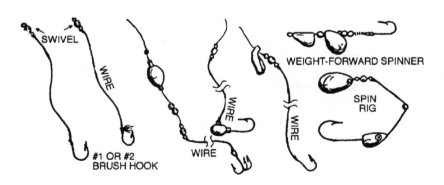

## FISH SPECIES

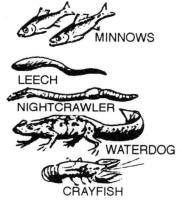

MINNOWS

LEECH

NIGHTCRAWLER

WATERDOG

CRAYFISH

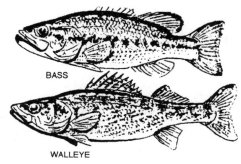

BASS

WALLEYE

## BAITS TO USE

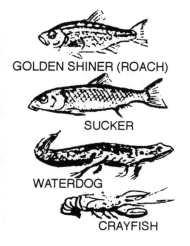

GOLDEN SHINER (ROACH)

SUCKER

WATERDOG

CRAYFISH

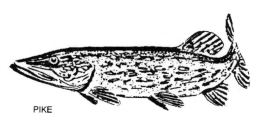

PIKE

**229**

## MORE BASIC FRESHWATER BAIT RIGS

RIGS

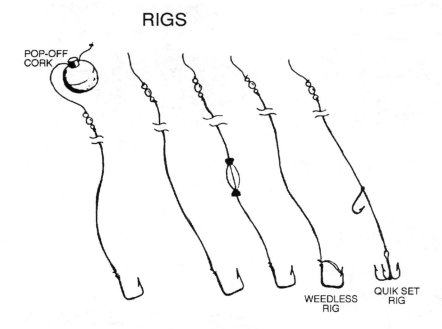

POP-OFF
CORK

WEEDLESS
RIG

QUIK SET
RIG

# FISH SPECIES

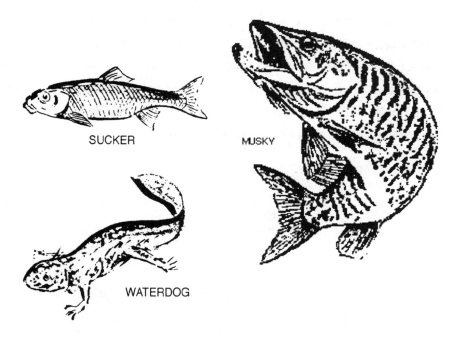

SUCKER

MUSKY

WATERDOG

# BAITS TO USE

**231**

## "FLOATING" BOTTOM WALKER RIG

This is an excellent natural bait rig for slow trolling and drifting in freshwater and saltwater, especially on rocky bottoms, oyster bars, or in areas having stumps and logs. Commercial "bottom walkers" in various weights are available from many tackle companies, including Lindy, which makes the "Bottom Cruiser." The beauty of this rig is that the lead weight of the "cruiser" walks along bottom, while the leader and bait are suspended off the bottom due to the addition of a small piece of foam that is threaded onto the leader. The Lindy "Float" is a good one that comes in many colors which adds to the rig's fish attracting quality.

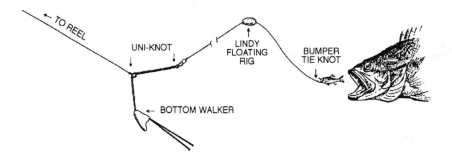

## "DROPPER" ICE RIG

This is an excellent terminal arrangement for ice fishermen to vertically present a pair of different weight lures to sportfish, especially panfish. The ice fishing spoon keeps the line taut, so bites are most noticeable. The small wet fly or nymph is positioned several feet above the spoon, and is deadly for suspended fish. A loop-type knot for the ice fishing spoon is best because it allows the lure to have the most action during jigging. Both lures can be made more effective by "tipping" them with a small natural bait, such as fly larva, or with a commercial scent product such as Berkley's "Power Wigglers" or "Crappie Nibbles."

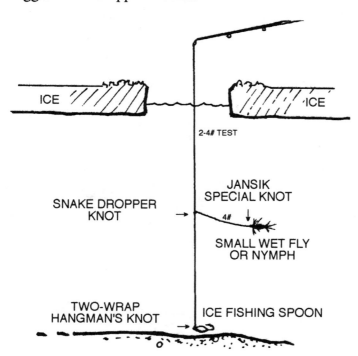

ICE

ICE

2-4# TEST

JANSIK
SPECIAL KNOT

SNAKE DROPPER
KNOT

4#

SMALL WET FLY
OR NYMPH

TWO-WRAP
HANGMAN'S KNOT

ICE FISHING SPOON

**233**

## BASIC BOBBER BAIT RIGS

These most basic terminal tackle set-ups for fishing natural baits have probably accounted for more fish than all other lure and bait rigs combined. All that's needed are a float, split shot, hook or small jig. It's usually best to position the split shot 6- to 18-inches above the bait, which prevents spooking fish. The depth the bait is fished is determined by where the bobber is positioned on the fishing line. Normally, it's best to set the bobber so the bait hovers about 1-foot off bottom. When large "meaty" baits like minnows are fished from a float, a treble hook often is preferred because striking fish are most surely barbed. For long, slender baits such as nightcrawler worms and leeches, a single hook, such as a jig head, is effective. For added action with a jig head, use a "loop" type knot when tying to the rig's leader.

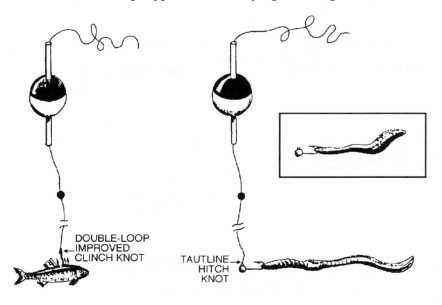

DOUBLE-LOOP
←IMPROVED
CLINCH KNOT

TAUTLINE→
HITCH
KNOT

*Stream trout fishermen should know how to properly design and taper their fly leaders.*

## WIRE RIGS FOR NATURAL BAIT

These versatile live bait rigs can be used in saltwater or freshwater, and they can be made with single hooks, treble hooks, short-shank hooks, offset-shank hooks and other hook styles. Some anglers also rig hooks with split rings, believing that such rigs are less likely to bind and break during fights with strong, toothy fish. The rigs shown are made with single-strand wire, preferably coffee-colored, and all connections are made with Haywire Twists. Multi-strand wire also can be used, but crimps must then be employed.

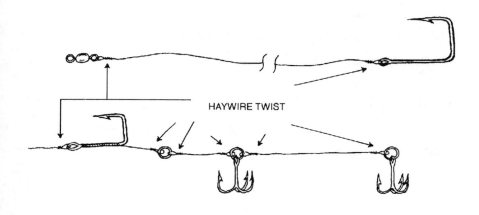

HAYWIRE TWIST

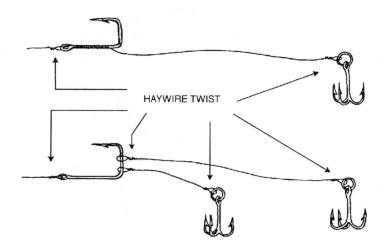

HAYWIRE TWIST

**237**

## JIG AND "SWEETNER"

Almost any leadhead jig can be made more effective by adding a "sweetner" of natural bait.  In freshwater, a leech, crawfish, nightcrawler, minnow, or even a strip of fish flesh (skin on) will make any jig more appealing to fish.  In saltwater, tipping a jig with a fresh shrimp, squid, small baitfish, piece of conch or fresh-cut strip of fish flesh works well, too. For most jig styles, a loop type knot is best, as a jig will "swim" more enticingly to attract sportfish, especially when there's a "sweetner" trailing it.

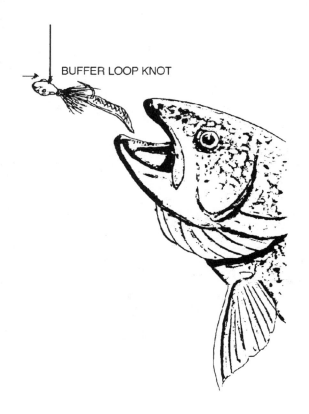

BUFFER LOOP KNOT

## FIXED LEADER RIGS

These two rigs have a set or "fixed" length between the hook and weight. The "higher" you want the bait off bottom the longer the leader that must be used. For example, if on your fathometer you're "marking" fish suspended 6-feet off the lake floor, a 6- to 8-foot long leader should be employed, which will position your bait where fish are holding. Long leaders also can be used to keep baits above weeds, jagged rocks, stumps and flooded timber. If you use a small cork or float on the leader to keep a bait off bottom, position it at least 6-inches ahead of the bait. The Lindy Walking Sinker is good for fishing most bottom types, while the bullet sinker set-up is best in weeds.

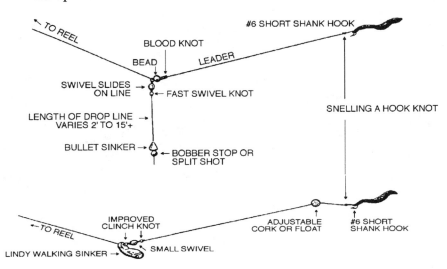

**239**

## WEEDLESS NATURAL BAIT RIG

This is one of the simplest and best ways to fish a natural bait in weeds, rocks and flooded timber. All that's needed are a weedless hook, a bullet-shaped slip sinker and a bait. Slide the sinker onto the fishing line, tie on the hook, and barb the bait. Some anglers like to "pin" the sinker to the hook eye with a toothpick. This is done simply by wedging the toothpick in the sinker hook against the fishing line, then trimming the toothpick close to the sinker. This in effect makes the rig much like a jig. It's effective in saltwater and freshwater, and many types of natural baits can be used, such as minnows, leeches, nightcrawlers, shrimp, squid, eels, etc.

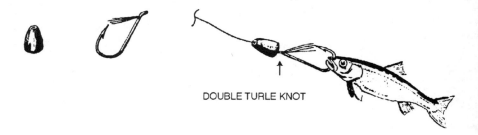

DOUBLE TURLE KNOT

## STANDARD WIRE LEADER

While commercially-made wire leaders are available almost everywhere, and some are well designed, many veteran anglers prefer to make their own because it's so simple to do. Single-strand wire is preferred, in brown or black, because it's less visible to fish than silver wire. The size and length wire is dependant on the style fishing and the fish sought. Usually, a leader 1- to 3-feet long is ample. A good quality all-black, ball-bearing, barrel swivel is at the leader's head, with a black snap or snap-swivel at the leader end. Haywire Twists are used to secure all single-strand wire connections.

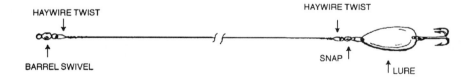

HAYWIRE TWIST

HAYWIRE TWIST

BARREL SWIVEL

SNAP

LURE

## DEEP TROLLING LURE/BAIT RIG

This is an excellent trolling rig for getting lures and baits deep for lake trout, walleyes, bass, stripers and in saltwater for redfish, snook, flounder and seatrout. A heavy bead-chain or "keel" sinker is fastened to the fishing line, then attached to one ring of a 3-way swivel. Next, a short leader is rigged to a diving plug off another ring of the 3-way swivel. Finally, a longer leader is fitted to the 3-way swivel and to a spinner natural bait rig. This spinner can be fitted with a nightcrawler for fish like walleyes, or with a strip of fish flesh for flounder or lake trout. The beauty of this deep trolling rig is that it allows anglers to simultaneously offer fish a lure **and** a flashy natural bait. Don't be surprised to hook two fish at once with this rig.

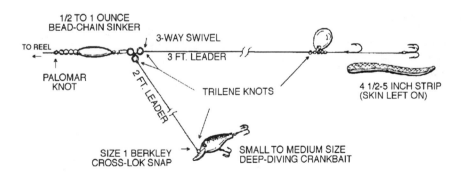

**242**

## JIG AND FLY RIG FOR PANFISH

This is one of the most deadly rigs for panfish ever devised. At times bluegills, crappies, white bass and others find two lures more appealing than one. Also, the plastic-bodied jig provides the rig with excellent "up-and-down" action as an angler imparts movement to it with his rod tip. The small fly frequently is the most effective panfish lure in the rig, but only can be cast because the heavier jig has been added. If additional casting weight is needed, or if deep water must be worked, a bullet-shaped slip-sinker can be added to the fishing line above the 3-way swivel.

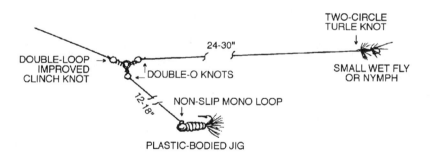

DOUBLE-LOOP IMPROVED CLINCH KNOT
24-30"
DOUBLE-O KNOTS
TWO-CIRCLE TURLE KNOT
SMALL WET FLY OR NYMPH
12-18"
NON-SLIP MONO LOOP
PLASTIC-BODIED JIG

**243**

## KENTUCKY LAKE CRAPPIE RIG

Crappies are well known for "suspending," and that makes them especially difficult for some anglers to catch. The Kentucky Lake Crappie Rig was developed on the sprawling mid-south impoundment, and addresses the "suspended fish" problem by positioning baits a couple feet off bottom. In deep, flooded timber, sometimes adding three, four or even five baits is most effective in locating the depth where a school of crappies is holding. Also, some anglers use jigs, or jig-and-minnow combinations on this rig. If using jigs, try several different color lures to learn if the fish have a color preference on a particular day.

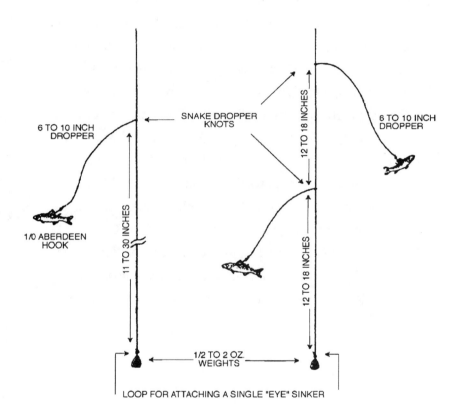

6 TO 10 INCH
DROPPER

SNAKE DROPPER
KNOTS

6 TO 10 INCH
DROPPER

12 TO 18 INCHES

1/0 ABERDEEN
HOOK

11 TO 30 INCHES

12 TO 18 INCHES

1/2 TO 2 OZ.
WEIGHTS

LOOP FOR ATTACHING A SINGLE "EYE" SINKER

**245**

## CAROLINA RIG

This innovative rig has become one of the most popular ways to fish soft plastic lures for bass. It also can be used with floating-diving plugs and natural baits. The Carolina Rig allows anglers to cover water faster than if a standard bottom-bumping lure were used. Also, the Carolina Rig is excellent for deep-water fishing, and can be trolled or drifted. Recently some important modifications have been developed for the rig which incorporates fish-appealing sound to the lure. By using a heavy brass slip weight, glass bead and brass barrel swivel, each time the brass parts hit the glass bead a sharp "clack" is made, which draws the attention of fish. This is a real plus in deep or muddy water. For clear water, using a small plastic worm with exposed hooks makes the Carolina Rig very effective. Leader length determines how "high" the lure floats above bottom. In places with tall weeds or brush use a long leader, where weeds and moss are minimal try a shorter leader.

**246**

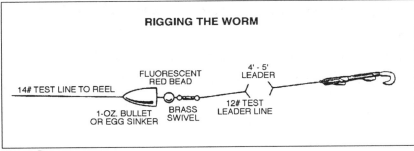

**RIGGING THE WORM**

14# TEST LINE TO REEL

FLUORESCENT
RED BEAD

4' - 5'
LEADER

1-OZ. BULLET
OR EGG SINKER

BRASS
SWIVEL

12# TEST
LEADER LINE

**247**

## TEXAS RIG

This is the most popular and one of the best ways to make a soft plastic lure. Plastic worms, lizards, grubs, tubes, crawfish, almost anything can be rigged this way and made virtually weedless. One important key to this rig is to position the hook point so it is **almost** exposed through the worm. With the hook this way, it can be "driven" through the plastic and into a fish's mouth with a minimum of force at the hook set. Some anglers prefer to use a brass bullet sinker and add a glass bead positioned between the worm and the sinker on the fishing line. The sinker striking the bead produces a loud clicking sound which gets the attention of fish.

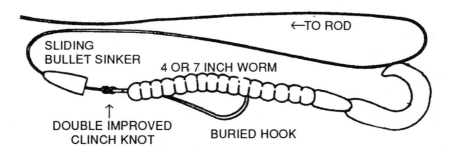

←TO ROD

SLIDING
BULLET SINKER

4 OR 7 INCH WORM

↑
DOUBLE IMPROVED
CLINCH KNOT

BURIED HOOK

**248**

## WEEDLESS BASS BAIT RIGS

Shiners and frogs are two of the best live baits for bass. A standard weedless hook should be used, and baits should hooked as shown in the illustration. For floating weeds, a weedless hook should be placed in a shiner **under** the bait, just forward of the tail fin. A low-profile, torpedo-shaped float should be used because it "works" through weeds with ease, which prevents break offs from bass.

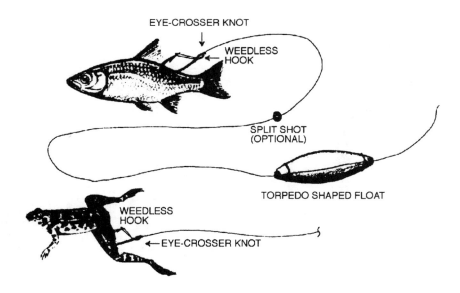

EYE-CROSSER KNOT

WEEDLESS HOOK

SPLIT SHOT (OPTIONAL)

TORPEDO SHAPED FLOAT

WEEDLESS HOOK

←EYE-CROSSER KNOT

**249**

## SLIP-FLOAT RIGGING

Slip-floats are designed to slide along the fishing line, and can be "set" to fish a bait or lure at any desired depth. A "Stop Knot" or "float stop" is positioned on the fishing line, above the slip float. After a cast is made the "Stop Knot" halts at the top of the slip float, which stops line from flowing through the float and thus determines the depth the bait or lure is fished. The beauty of a slip float is that a bait or lure can be fished at any depth, which is pre-set simply by sliding the "Stop Knot" closer to or farther away from the slip float. Another plus is that slip floats are easily cast with spinning, spin-cast and bait-casting tackle.

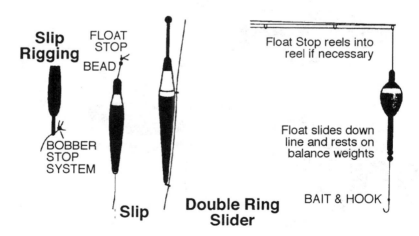

Slip Rigging
FLOAT STOP
BEAD
BOBBER STOP SYSTEM
Slip
Double Ring Slider

Float Stop reels into reel if necessary

Float slides down line and rests on balance weights

BAIT & HOOK

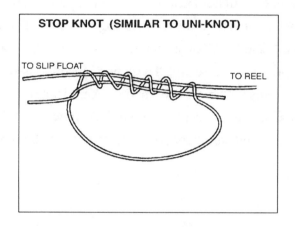

**STOP KNOT (SIMILAR TO UNI-KNOT)**

TO SLIP FLOAT

TO REEL

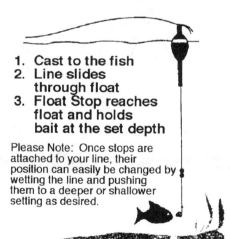

1. Cast to the fish
2. Line slides through float
3. Float Stop reaches float and holds bait at the set depth

Please Note: Once stops are attached to your line, their position can easily be changed by wetting the line and pushing them to a deeper or shallower setting as desired.

**251**

## "HOLD BACK" RIGGING FOR MODERN FLOATS IN CURRENT

Current speed in many rivers and in tidewaters is often twice as fast at the surface as it is at the bottom. This is why most fish in current hold near bottom. When a modern American surface float is used for river fishing it's imperative that the float is "held back" or substantially slowed so baits and lures are presented correctly. These two illustrations show proven systems to "hold back" modern American floats in current, and are favorites of Mick Thill, designer of Thill fishing floats, and an international match fishing champion.

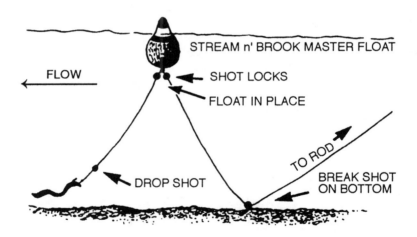

FLOW

STREAM n' BROOK MASTER FLOAT

SHOT LOCKS

FLOAT IN PLACE

TO ROD

DROP SHOT

BREAK SHOT ON BOTTOM

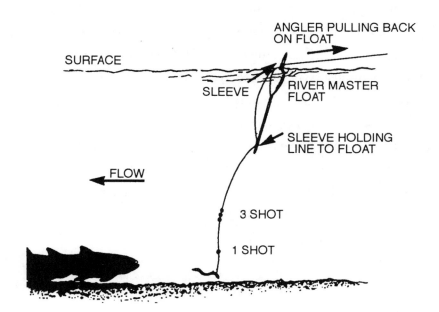

ANGLER PULLING BACK
ON FLOAT

SURFACE

SLEEVE

RIVER MASTER
FLOAT

SLEEVE HOLDING
LINE TO FLOAT

FLOW

3 SHOT

1 SHOT

**253**

## FISH-FINDER RIG

This bottom rig can be used for a wide variety of fish in many different situations.  It's a favorite among surf, pier and jetty fishermen when a pyramid sinker is employed.  With a pyramid sinker, the rig will not tumble along bottom.  Yet, when a fish picks up the bait and moves off with it, it can pull the bait away from the sinker unimpeded.  Be certain the leader test is lighter than the fishing line, so if the bait becomes fouled and must be pulled free by the angler, only the hook and leader are lost, not the entire rig.

A fish-finder rig also can be made with a barrel, egg or bank-style sinker that has a hole through it.  Such sinkers tumble or roll along bottom in strong current, which can be desirable should the angler want the bait to cover a lot of area, provided the bottom is hard-packed sand and the hook and bait are not likely to foul.

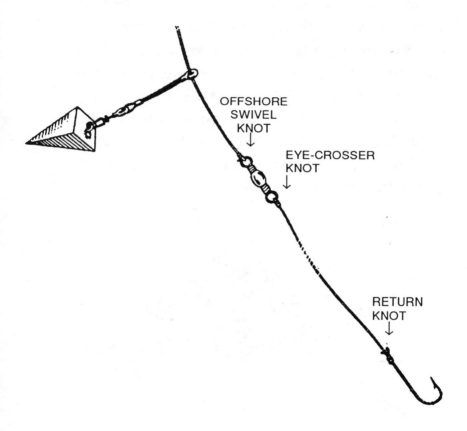

OFFSHORE
SWIVEL
KNOT
↓

EYE-CROSSER
KNOT
↓

RETURN
KNOT
↓

## RIGGING FOR SKEE FISHING

A modern Great Lakes salmon and trout trolling boat has rods and lines projecting out in all directions, looking more like a huge spider walking on water than an efficient fishing machine. Such boats make use of port and starboard "skees," which can spread lines and lures up to 100 feet to each side of the boat. Such a trolling set up allows anglers to cover a great deal of water, and thus present lures to more fish in less time. Rigging for "skee fishing" takes a bit of effort, but it's simple, very efficient angling that works in freshwater and saltwater. Companies such as Wille Products make special "skee" masts, lines and release mechanisms that are well made and help make trolling more pleasurable and efficient.

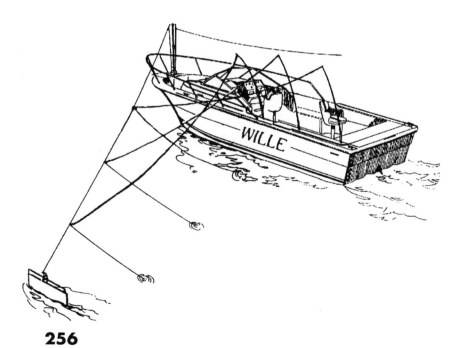

## LINE RELEASE

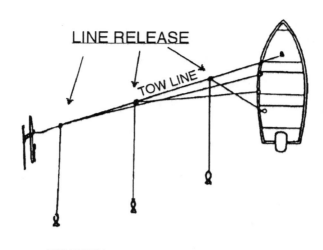

TOW LINE

TOW ROPE
125'

LEFT
(PORT)
BOARD

RIGHT
(STARBOARD)
BOARD

#3 IS
UNDER
#2 AND
#1

#2 IS
UNDER
#1

#1

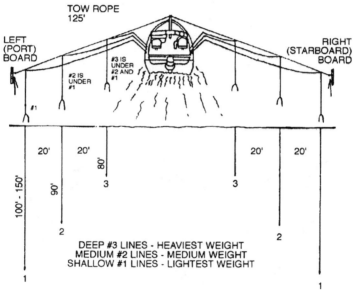

20'   20'   20'   20'

100' - 150'   90'   80'

3   3

2   2

1   1

DEEP #3 LINES - HEAVIEST WEIGHT
MEDIUM #2 LINES - MEDIUM WEIGHT
SHALLOW #1 LINES - LIGHTEST WEIGHT

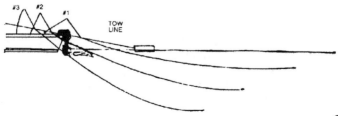

#3   #2   #1

TOW
LINE

**257**

## RIGGING FOR IN-LINE PLANERS

Anglers in small boats can enjoy much of the same benefits of "skee fishing" without large masts and heavy lines by employing "in-line" planers. Such planers work much like larger "skees," except they attach directly to an angler's fishing line. When set in the "troll" position, the in-line planer pulls away from a trolling boat, which takes the fisherman's lure or bait with it. The distance the planer runs from the boat is determined by how much fishing line the angler releases from his reel. When a fish strikes, the board "trips" and the fish is fought as usual without much interference from the in-line planer.

The benefits of "in-line" planer boards are that they are inexpensive, very portable, and allow trollers to cover wide areas quickly and efficiently.

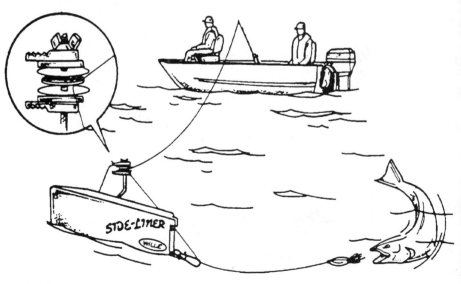

## BIG GAME FLY LEADER

There are many different variations of tying a fly leader capable of handling everything from sharks and tarpon to sailfish and marlin. This basic big game leader is simple, and casts well because it's short and tapers quickly. For most big game fly-rodding, leaders need not be long, about 6 to 8 feet. The leader butt typically is 3- to 4-feet long. The butt ends in a loop, so that ready-made leader tippets can be quickly fastened to the butt when fly type or color, or tippet weight, must be changed.

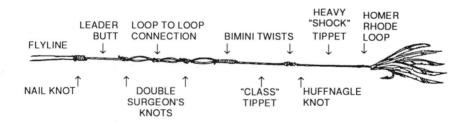

HEAVY "SHOCK" TIPPET — HOMER RHODE LOOP — LEADER BUTT — LOOP TO LOOP CONNECTION — BIMINI TWISTS — FLYLINE

NAIL KNOT — DOUBLE SURGEON'S KNOTS — "CLASS" TIPPET — HUFFNAGLE KNOT

## CHRISTMAS TREE BOTTOM RIG

This is a fast, very effective method of vertically fishing bottom baits. It's used primarily by grouper and snapper fishermen, but it also works well for deep water crappies, walleyes, perch, whitefish and sauger. It's important to use heavy, stiff monofilament in the rig, as this prevents bait tangles. The hook closest to the sinker is designed to be rigged with a small live baitfish, while the other "droppers" are set-up for dead baits or "strip baits." Live baits can be used from the droppers, however, longer distances of at least 18 inches should be made between dropper leaders to prevent live baits from tangling.

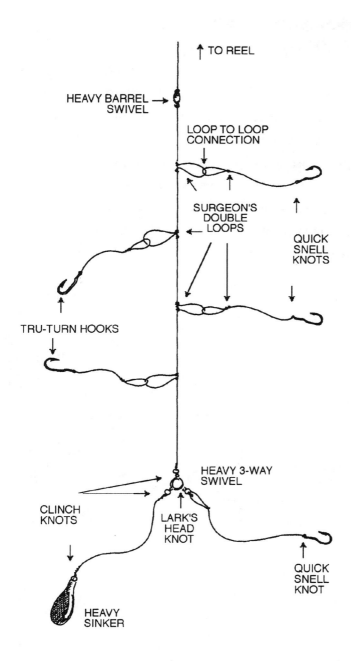

TO REEL

HEAVY BARREL → SWIVEL

LOOP TO LOOP CONNECTION

SURGEON'S DOUBLE LOOPS

QUICK SNELL KNOTS

TRU-TURN HOOKS

HEAVY 3-WAY SWIVEL

CLINCH KNOTS

LARK'S HEAD KNOT

QUICK SNELL KNOT

HEAVY SINKER

## SPLIT-SHOT AND FLOATING GRUB

This is a very simple and excellent way to get small, floating plastic-tail grubs deep for spooky, clear-water bass, crappies, walleyes and trout. Use small, light-wire hooks and light-test line, which helps keep the grub buoyant. In clear water, yellow, white and smoke-colored grubs are deadly. All-black grubs also work well, especially for smallmouths, because they imitate leeches. This rig is a good one to fish slowly over deep rock piles, grass-bottom areas and moss beds, because the floating grub flutters enticingly off the bottom above the split-shot.

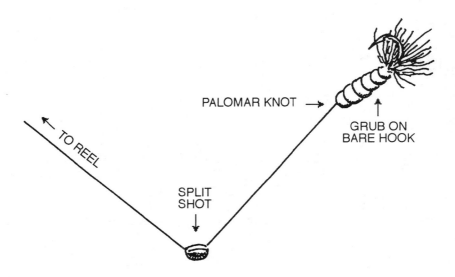

## FLOATING GRUB "DROPPER" RIG

This is a great way to quickly locate the depth panfish, bass, walleyes and other sportfish are suspended. A series of dropper lines with floating grubs attached can be "stacked" above the split shot, and when one lure at one depth starts to draw strikes, that's the depth level to concentrate your efforts. Also, by "stacking" **floating** grubs with this rig, several different color and style models can be used to learn which is best for that day on the water. This is a dynamite crappie rig for vertical fishing in flooded timber. Keep dropper lines short to prevent tangling.

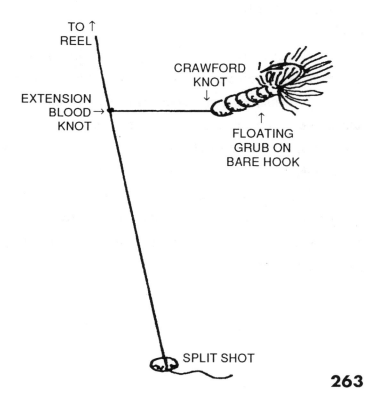

TO ↑
REEL

CRAWFORD
KNOT
↓

EXTENSION
BLOOD →
KNOT

FLOATING
GRUB ON
BARE HOOK
↑

SPLIT SHOT

**263**

## DOWNRIGGER AND PLANER RIG

In recent years some innovative anglers have learned that by combining downriggers and deep planers they have more accurate control over their trolled lures, particularly when using artificials or dead baits at high boat speeds.

In most trolling situations where the boat is moving faster than three knots, anglers have come to learn that when a downrigger counter indicates a bait trolled under the boat is worked at 50 feet, "blow back" actually positions the bait at half the indicated depth—in this case 25 feet. So, with "blow back," a downrigger counter would have to indicate the bait is trolled at 100 feet in order to effectively reach the 50 foot level.

But by combining downriggers with deep-going planers, a better, more precise way of trolling can be achieved.

Basically, all that is done in this style fishing is to attach a deep-going planer to a downrigger cannonball. A simple release clip is fitted to the back of the deep planer, and to this release clip is attached the fishing line.

In use, the downrigger and deep planer are lowered to the desired depth. The depth indicated on the downrigger counter will be very accurate, because the deep planer keeps the cannonball deep, thereby eliminating "blow back."

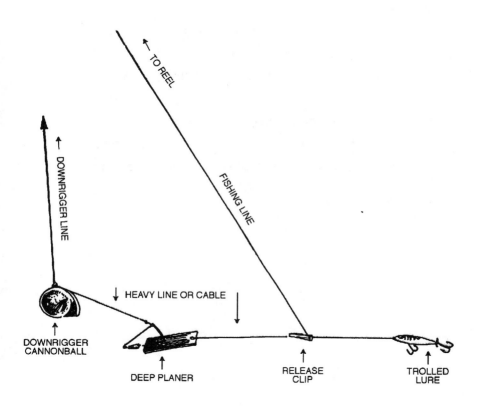

TO REEL

DOWNRIGGER LINE

FISHING LINE

HEAVY LINE OR CABLE

DOWNRIGGER
CANNONBALL

DEEP PLANER

RELEASE
CLIP

TROLLED
LURE

## MULTIPLE DROPPER RIG

This is a popular surf rig used by pompano fishermen who bait their hooks with sand fleas and small pieces of shrimp or squid. This also is a good rig for small bluefish, Spanish mackerel and red drum. It's a good idea to have leaders of lighter pound test than the main line of the rig so if a hook fouls only that line will be lost, not the whole rig. This rig is easy and fast to make, and can be changed quickly because of the snap swivel at the top. Also, should water depth or current conditions change, heavier or lighter weights can be added. Wire leaders also can be used, but they must have snap swivels that can be attached to the dropper loops.

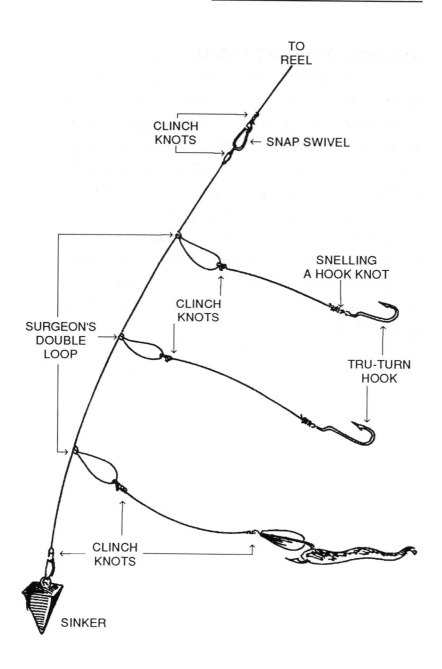

TO
REEL

CLINCH
KNOTS

SNAP SWIVEL

SNELLING
A HOOK KNOT

CLINCH
KNOTS

SURGEON'S
DOUBLE
LOOP

TRU-TURN
HOOK

CLINCH
KNOTS

SINKER

## RIGGING WIRE LINE FOR TROLLING

Many modern anglers disdain using wire line for trolling. But because downrigger cannonballs foul in rocky or irregular bottoms, wire line still is an important method for anglers to get lures and baits deep in some fishing situations. How much wire line to rig into a trolling line is dependent on how fast and deep anglers troll. The longer the length of wire and the heavier its gauge, the deeper it runs. This rig is an excellent one when wire lines are mandated, but anglers must use the trial-and-error method to learn how much wire is needed in the line to correctly present lures to fish. The trolling sinker in this rig can be varied in weight to help reach different depths.

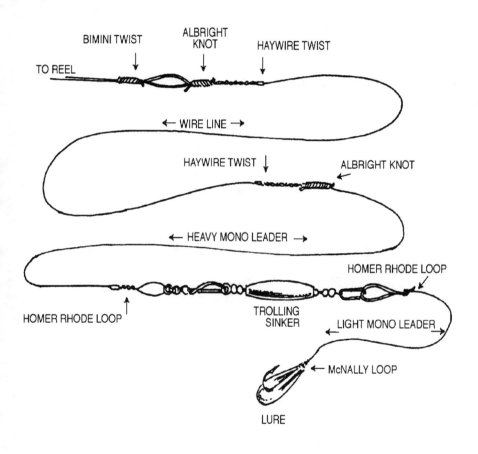

BIMINI TWIST · ALBRIGHT KNOT · HAYWIRE TWIST

TO REEL

← WIRE LINE →

HAYWIRE TWIST ↓ · ALBRIGHT KNOT

← HEAVY MONO LEADER →

HOMER RHODE LOOP

HOMER RHODE LOOP

TROLLING SINKER

LIGHT MONO LEADER →

← McNALLY LOOP

LURE

## TANDEM HOOK DEAD BAIT RIG

Two hooks are often better than one for catching many gamefish species, and that's especially true when large, "meaty" marine baits are used such as mullet, giant squid, and Spanish mackerel. Even in freshwater, when big suckers or ciscos are fished for muskies and pike, 2-hook bait rigs make plenty of sense.

While this tandem-hook dead bait rig is designed primarily for marine fishing, it also works well in the freshwater arena when pike, muskies and even huge lake trout are the targets.

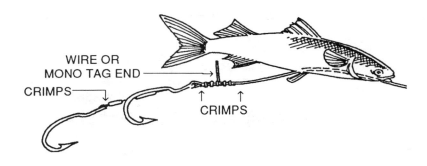

WIRE OR
MONO TAG END

CRIMPS

CRIMPS

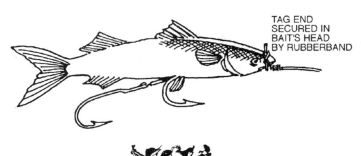

TAG END
SECURED IN
BAIT'S HEAD
BY RUBBERBAND

# 8

## Good Knots and Playing Fish Right

All other factors equal, knots are the weakest part of any fishing system. However, when the proper knot is used for a specific angling situation, and the knot is properly tied, a fisherman may fight a hooked fish to the limits of his tackle and be confident in the knowledge that "all will hold."

Many fishermen have little understanding of the extreme pressures their fishing tackle can take. It doesn't matter if the fishing gear is fly, spinning, spin-cast or bait-casting. If it's rigged right, and good knots are tied, the tackle will take a lot of punishment before anything gives.

Seasoned fishermen are familiar with the amount of strain each of their fishing outfits will take. They know, for example, precisely how much pressure can be applied with a particular rod and line before one or the other breaks.

To familiarize yourself with the built-in "power" of your fishing outfits, tie their lines to a stationary object. Then, holding the rod at about the 3:00 o'clock position, tighten up and raise the rod. Keep putting a deep bend in the rod, and actually try to break the line. Do not snap the rod back and up. Just apply a strong, steady, upward pull. Unless you've got very light line, or have tied poor knots, you'll find that everything holds and that, in fact, you most likely cannot break the

*Leave about a rod's length of line out as you're about to land a fish, then "draw" it to you by bringing the rod tip straight back.*

line no matter how hard you try. Such tests will show how tough your tackle is, and that there is no need to "baby" fish you hook.

In learning to tie knots included in this book, it's worthwhile to test them as described above. Let's say, for example, you've made a fly fishing leader using Blood Knots to connect the various leader strands, a Nail Knot to connect the leader butt to the fly line, and an Improved Clinch Knot to tie the leader tippet to a fly. Set up your fly outfit, and hook the fly onto something solid. Now start to pull. If all the knots have been tied properly, you'll discover it is impossible to break the leader or to pull out a knot, unless of course, the leader tippet is super fine, testing a couple pounds or less.

The same kind of knot testing should be done with other tackle. Experienced tarpon fishermen, for example, do not make a cast until they've checked their tackle. Tarpon are a tremendous test of a fisherman's gear, and of how well he can tie knots. So most tarpon anglers, after having rigged up, attach their hooks to something solid, and then **pull, pull, pull**—and **pull** some more. When they're convinced everything will hold, they go fishing. Not before.

Fish that are hooked, no matter what the species, never should be "babied," but neither should they be "horsed." "Babying" is handling a fish so fearfully, so gently, that the fish barely exerts any pressure against the tackle. "Horsing" is doing it the other way around, pulling on the fish so hard it

**273**

doesn't have a chance to fight. The fisherman who consistently "horses" fish he hooks is going to lose most of the good ones he gets on. Applying too much pressure too soon to a good fish is going to cause the hooks to pull out, line or rod to break, or a knot to slip if it wasn't tied correctly.

Hooked fish should be fought according to their size and power, and according to the breaking point of the tackle. Skilled anglers fighting a fish strong enough to tax their tackle, "play" the fish right up to just short of the breaking point of their gear. Knowing how much strain their rod, reel, line and knots will stand, they are able to fight a fish to the "tackle maximum."

Knowing how to play hooked fish is as important as rigging tackle correctly and tying knots fastidiously. It will do little good to become an expert fisherman and a knot-tying and rig-making genius, only to lose big fish at the boat because of some carelessness in playing them.

The first step in getting any fish into the boat is to set the hook properly. A lot of beginning fishermen, and some old-timers as well, do not understand that hooks must be "set" or driven past the barbs into fish, and that only rarely will a fish hook itself.

Use a rod that has enough backbone to sink hooks into fish when you pull back sharply on the rod as a fish strikes. In fishing for hard-mouth species—such as tarpon or muskies— use a rod with considerable backbone or stiffness. For soft-

**274**

mouth fish, such as walleyes, trout, crappies, etc., a rod with much lighter action can be used.

It takes a solid pull on a rod to sink hook barbs, and the larger the hooks used, the more difficult it is to set them properly in striking fish. The fishing line should be kept taut at all times, and the rod in a low position during retrieves. When a fish hits, the angler should raise his rod back swiftly and with authority in order to bury hooks past their barbs.

In some kinds of fishing, many anglers "set" hooks not once, but three, four, or more times. Hard-mouthed fish always should be struck by an angler several times. This includes muskies, tarpon, marlin and sailfish.

When a fish is hooked right, half the battle is won. But after hooking, a fish still must be played out and landed.

Never try to bring in a hooked fish by simply reeling. Instead, press the rod butt against your middle, and bring in line and the fish by the "pump-and-reel" method. To "pump" a fish, lower the rod tip and reel quickly to keep a tight line. Then raise the rod smoothly, which will bring the fish toward you. Keep pumping and reeling to draw the fish close, but when it wants to go on a strong run, let it go.

Always let the rod and reel do the work in fighting a fish. By pumping and reeling, the rod will bend and flex, and thus tire the fish. The natural give-and-take action of a rod wears a fish down. The drag on a reel also serves to beat strong fish. When a hooked fish scoots away taking line, it must pull against the reel's drag, and that can quickly exhaust it.

Try to keep fish from running out too much line. The more line between you and the fish you've hooked, the less control you have in fighting it. Also, with a relatively short line, you can exert maximum pressure on a fish during the fight.

A fish hooked well should not get loose in open water, even if slack line is given. However, a fish getting slack near roots, weeds or stumps can break off quickly. Always keep a firm, tight line when fighting fish near snags. Whenever you hook a fish in weedy or snag-filled water, try to work it into the open quickly.

Give slack line when hooked fish jump, especially if it's a large one on light line. If you don't lower the rod tip and give slack when a big fish jumps, it might fall on a tight line and either break the line or pull out the hooks.

When hooked fish are brought close, they normally spook and make a last ditch run. Be ready for it. If the fish makes a final, strong charge, let it go. It'll normally only run a short distance, pause, and you can bring it right back again for landing.

When fish are properly played out they will lay on one side, right at the surface, fins fluttering weakly. They may be gently released then, or landed by netting, gaffing or grasping by hand. Never put your fingers under the gill plate of a fish to be released, since this could injure it seriously.

Bass, crappies and small trout can be landed easily by placing a thumb in the mouth, pressing down, then lifting. Such a grip temporarily paralyzes them, and they will not struggle. Muskies, pike and walleyes have needle-like teeth, so are best landed by "collaring" from above, just behind the gill plates.

When preparing to boat a fish, leave a bit more than a rod's length of line out, then ease the fish to you by raising the rod up and back. If the fish doesn't come in readily, it is not worn out enough. Let it go off again, and let the rod's action wear it down more.

When using a landing net, place it in the water and lead the fish into it head first. Never make quick, sweeping moves at a hooked fish with a net. All this will do is spook it into a darting run, and the fish may break free.

Regardless of how skillfully you hook and play fish, or how perfectly you tie knots and construct fishing rigs, you are going to lose some. It's part of the game—the great game of fishing.

*Captain Ray Henley holds a pair of spunky bluefish he caught on one plug. He made the catch because his knot system held despite the "double header."*

# Index

**Symbols**

100 PERCENT KNOT  *SEE* BIMINI TWIST
20-SECOND NAIL KNOT  *SEE* FAST NAIL KNOT
20-TIMES AROUND KNOT  *SEE* BIMINI TWIST
3-WAY SWIVEL DEEP RIG    219

**A**

ALBRIGHT SPECIAL KNOT    44
ANGLER'S KNOT    19, 166
ARBOR KNOT    118
ATTACHING LEADER TO LINE    32

**B**

BALLYHOO RIG    200
BARREL KNOT    37
BARREL TWIST  *SEE* OVERHAND WIRE WRAP
BASIC BOBBER BAIT RIGS    234
BASIC FRESHWATER BAIT RIGS    228
BERKLEY TRILENE KNOT    64
BIG GAME CABLE LOOP  *SEE* CIRCLE WRAP WITH DOUBLE
    SLEEVE
BIG GAME FLY LEADER    259
BIMINI TWIST    120
BLOOD DROPPER LOOP  *SEE* DROPPER LOOP
BLOOD KNOT    22, 178
BOTTOM RIG    208
BOW KNOT    70
BOWLINE KNOT    134
BRUBAKER KNOT    108
BUFFER LOOP KNOT    68, 168
BUMPER-TIE KNOT    60

## C

CADENAS KNOT    96
CAROLINA RIG    246
CHRISTMAS TREE BOTTOM RIG    260
CIRCLE WRAP WITH DOUBLE SLEEVE    200
CLINCH KNOT    83
CLINCH ON SHANK KNOT    98
COAT HANGER BAIT RIG FOR REEF FISHING    224
COMMON LOOP KNOT *SEE* SINGLE OVERHAND LOOP KNOT
COMPOSITE KNOT    45
COMPOUND KNOT    67
COMPOUND KNOT *SEE ALSO* PERFECTION LOOP
CRAWFORD KNOT    104
CROTCH SPLICE    135

## D

DAVE HAWK'S DROP-LOOP KNOT    84
DEEP TROLLING LURE/BAIT RIG    242
DEEP TROLLING RIG    220
DEEP TROLLING SPOON AND WIRE LEADER    207
DOUBLE BECKET BEND KNOT    38
DOUBLE EYE KNOT    90
DOUBLE FISHERMAN'S KNOT *SEE* DOUBLE WATER LOOP
    KNOT
DOUBLE HITCH JAM KNOT *SEE* CADENAS KNOT
DOUBLE IMPROVED CLINCH KNOT    50
DOUBLE JAM KNOT *SEE* BERKLEY TRILENE KNOT
DOUBLE LINE HALF-HITCH KNOT    68
DOUBLE LOOP IMPROVED CLINCH KNOT *SEE* IMPROVED
    BERKLEY TRILENE KNOT
DOUBLE NAIL KNOT    156
DOUBLE NAIL-KNOT LOOP    141
DOUBLE OVERHAND JAM KNOT *SEE* CADENAS KNOT
DOUBLE OVERHAND KNOT *SEE* SURGEON'S LOOP
DOUBLE SALMON KNOTS *SEE* DOUBLE SNELL KNOTS
DOUBLE SHEET BEND KNOT    94
DOUBLE SNELL KNOTS    98
DOUBLE SURGEON'S LOOP *SEE* SURGEON'S LOOP

DOUBLE TURLE KNOT    144
DOUBLE WATER KNOT *SEE* SURGEON'S KNOT
DOUBLE WATER LOOP KNOT    42
DOUBLE WEMYSS KNOT    76
DOUBLE-LOOP CLINCH KNOT *SEE* BERKLEY TRILENE
    KNOT
DOUBLE-O KNOT    53
DOUBLE-SLEEVE RIG    195
DOWNRIGGER AND PLANER RIG    264
"DROPPER" ICE RIG    233
DROPPER KNOT    12
DROPPER LOOP    130
DROPPER SNELL KNOT    35, 166
DUNCAN LOOP KNOT    52

**E**

EMERGENCY DROPPER KNOT    37
END LOOP KNOT    119
EXTENSION BLOOD KNOT    26, 180
EYE KNOT *SEE* DOUBLE-O KNOT
EYE-CROSSER KNOT    100

**F**

FAST NAIL KNOT    154
FAST SWIVEL KNOT    97
FEATHER-STRIP TROLLING RIG    227
FIGURE EIGHT KNOT    91, 199
FIGURE EIGHT KNOT *SEE ALSO* TWO-WRAP HANGMAN'S
    KNOT
FIGURE-EIGHT KNOT    32
FISH-FINDER RIG    254
FISHERMAN'S BEND KNOT    13
FISHERMEN'S LOOP *SEE* PERFECTION LOOP
FIXED LEADER RIGS    239
FLEMISH LOOP *SEE* HOMER RHODE LOOP KNOT
"FLOATING" BOTTOM WALKER RIG    232
FLOATING GRUB "DROPPER" RIG    263
FLY LINE LOOP    140

## H

HALF-BLOOD KNOT  *SEE* CLINCH KNOT
HAYWIRE TWIST      186
HEATED TWIST  *SEE* MATCH METHOD
HEAVY-DUTY FLY LEADER      205
HELM KNOT  *SEE* TILLER HITCH KNOT
HITCH KNOT  *SEE* TILLER HITCH KNOT
"HOLD BACK" RIGGING FOR MODERN FLOATS IN CURRENT
      252
HOMER RHODE LOOP KNOT      62
HOMER'S KNOT      110
HUFFNAGLE KNOT      182

## I

IMPROVED BERKLEY TRILENE KNOT      66
IMPROVED BLOOD KNOT      24
IMPROVED CLINCH KNOT      76, 170

## J

JAM HITCH  *SEE* JAM KNOT
JAM KNOT      30
JAM KNOT WITH AN EXTRA TUCK  *SEE* IMPROVED CLINCH
      KNOT
JANSIK SPECIAL KNOT      82
JIG AND FLY RIG FOR PANFISH      243
JIG AND "SWEETNER"      238
JOINER KNOT  *SEE* SURGEON'S KNOT
JOINING TWO LOOPS      39
JOINING WIRE TO FISHING LINE      189

## K

KENTUCKY LAKE CRAPPIE RIG      244
KEY KNOT SPLICE  *SEE* ALBRIGHT SPECIAL KNOT
KEY LOOP  *SEE* ALBRIGHT SPECIAL KNOT
KING SLING      58
KNOTTING BACKING TO FLY LINE      174
KNOTTING NYLON-COATED WIRE TO MONOFILAMENT

196

## L

LARK'S HEAD KNOT     81
LEADER DROPPER LOOP KNOT     34
LEADER KNOT     14
LEADER LOOP KNOT     124
LIGHT, FRESHWATER FLY LEADER     221
LINE KNOT *SEE* SURGEON'S LOOP
LOOP KNOT *SEE* HOMER RHODE LOOP KNOT

## M

MATCH METHOD     201
MCNALLY LOOP KNOT     74
METAL SLEEVE AND KNOT     194
METAL SLEEVE SECURING WIRE LOOP     190
MODIFIED NAIL KNOT     160
MULTIPLE CLINCH KNOT     17
MULTIPLE DROPPER RIG     266

## N

NAIL KNOT     150
NAIL KNOT USING HOOK     152
NAIL KNOT USING LINE-LOOP     152
NAIL LOOP KNOT     78
NEEDLE KNOT     164
NEEDLE NAIL KNOT     163
NEW ZEALAND OFFSHORE TROLLING RIG     215
NEWFOUNDLAND HITCH *SEE* PORTLAND CREEK HITCH

## O

OFFSET NAIL KNOT     158
OFFSHORE SWIVEL KNOT     102
OFFSHORE WIRE LEADER     222
OVERHAND DROPPER KNOT     36
OVERHAND EYE KNOT *SEE* SINGLE OVERHAND LOOP
    KNOT
OVERHAND KNOT WITH A KNOTTED END     38

OVERHAND WIRE WRAP     190

**P**

PALOMAR KNOT     54
PANDRE KNOT  *SEE* IMPROVED CLINCH KNOT
PENDRE DROPPER KNOT     40
PERFECTION LOOP     132
PERMANENT LOOP SPLICE IN DACRON     126
PINCH JAM  *SEE* JAM KNOT
PLUG WITH A SMALL TRAILING SPOON     226
POPPING CORK RIG     218
PORTLAND CREEK HITCH     148
PRIMA KNOT     85

**Q**

QUICK FLY LINE SPLICE     178
QUICK SNELL KNOT     92
QUICK-CHANGE WIRE WRAP     192

**R**

RAPALA KNOT     114
REEF KNOT  *SEE* SQUARE KNOT
RETURN JAM KNOT     88
RETURN KNOT     86
RIFFLING HITCH  *SEE* PORTLAND CREEK HITCH
RIG FOR CUT BAIT     188
RIGGING A BAITFISH FOR DEEP TROLLING     206
RIGGING A BALLYHOO FOR TROLLING     212
RIGGING A MONO LEADER TO BRAIDED LINE     214
RIGGING A MONO "SHOCK LEADER"     210
RIGGING FOR IN-LINE PLANERS     258
RIGGING FOR SKEE FISHING     256
RIGGING WIRE LINE FOR TROLLING     268
ROLLING SPLICE     176
ROLLOVER KNOT  *SEE* BIMINI TWIST
ROUND-TURN FISH HOOK TIE     71

# S

SAFETY-PIN RIG     193
SALMON HOOK KNOT *SEE* SNELLING A HOOK
SERRURE KNOT     56
SHOCKER KNOT     18, 172
SIMPLIFIED BLOOD KNOT     28
SINGLE FISHERMEN'S KNOT *SEE* ANGLER'S KNOT
SINGLE OVERHAND LOOP KNOT     129
SINGLE SHEET BEND KNOT     66
SINGLE WATER KNOT     42
SINGLE-SLEEVE RIG     188
SLIDING OVERHEAD KNOT     80
SLIP-FLOAT RIGGING     250
SLIPPED HITCH *SEE* TILLER HITCH KNOT
SNAKE DROPPER KNOT     43
SNELLING A HOOK     72
SPECIAL SPOON WRAP     198
SPECIALIST FLY KNOT     146
SPEED NAIL KNOT *SEE* FAST NAIL KNOT
SPIDER HITCH KNOT     136
SPLICED LOOP     176
SPLIT-SHOT AND FLOATING GRUB     262
SPLIT-SHOT SINKER LOOP     128
SPREADER RIG FOR NATURAL BAITS     216
SQUARE KNOT     45
STANDARD WIRE LEADER     241
STEVEDORE KNOT *SEE* CLINCH KNOT
STRIP-BAIT TROLLING RIG     217
SURGEON'S KNOT     31
SURGEON'S LOOP     129

# T

TANDEM HOOK DEAD BAIT RIG     270
TAUTLINE HITCH     79
TEXAS RIG     248
THE RAPALA KNOT     114
TILLER HITCH KNOT     21
TILLER KNOT *SEE* TILLER HITCH KNOT

TRIPLE FISHERMAN'S BEND KNOT    16
TROLLING SPOON WRAP *SEE* SPECIAL SPOON WRAP
TUBE KNOT *SEE* NAIL KNOT
TUCKED SHEET BEND KNOT    33
TURLE KNOT    142
TWO CIRCLE TURLE KNOT    106
TWO LURES ON A 3-WAY SWIVEL    211
TWO-FOLD BLOOD KNOT *SEE* SURGEON'S LOOP
TWO-FOLD WATER KNOT *SEE* SURGEON'S LOOP
TWO-RING SINKER LOOP    128
TWO-WRAP HANGMAN'S KNOT    94

## U

UNI-KNOT    46, 93
UNI-KNOT *SEE ALSO* DUNCAN LOOP KNOT

## V

VARIATION OF FISHERMAN'S BEND KNOT    16
VARIATION OF THE ANGLER'S KNOT    20
VARIATION OF THE NAIL KNOT    162

## W

WATER KNOT    41
WEEDLESS BASS BAIT RIGS    249
WEEDLESS NATURAL BAIT RIG    240
WHIP FINISH HOOK SNELL    116
WIRE RIGS FOR NATURAL BAIT    236
WOLF KNOT    40
WOLF SPLICE *SEE* WOLF KNOT
WORLD'S FAIR KNOT    112
WYSS TURLE KNOT    144